MW00626706

Youth
Soccer
Drills and Plays
Handbook

By Bob Swope
1st Edition 2008

After reading and using
this book:
"If you liked it and you think
it helped you, your team, or
parents your son or daughter,
tell all your friends and family
about it. "

Presented By:

Published and Distributed By:
Jacobob Press LLC
St. Louis, MO.
(314) 843-4829

Printed and Bound by:
No Waste Publishing
Fenton, MO.

First Edition 2008

*******WARNING*******

If your players or the participant has any physically limiting conditions, bleeding disorder, high blood pressure, pregnancy or any other condition that may limit them physically you should check with your doctor before letting them participate in any of these, drills or plays.

Be sure participants in these drills and plays that might make hard contact with any of the other participants are all approximately of the same weight and size to avoid a possible injury.

All the drills and plays for kids, should be supervised by an competent adult, coach, or a professional. **AUTHOR ASSUMES NO LIABILITY FOR ANY ACCIDENTAL INJURY OR EVEN DEATH THAT MAY RESULT.**

Extra care and caution should be taken with any of the various dribbling and heading drills and plays as they may be the more dangerous ones.

Bob Swope
Jacobob Press LLC
Publisher

TABLE OF CONTENTS

1. **Introduction** 6

2. **Drills, General Discussion** 7

3. **Plays, General Discussion** 7

4. **Strategy Discussion** 7
   Offensive 7
   Defensive 8

5. **Legend for Diagrams** 9

6. **Offensive Plays and Group Tactics** 9
   Individual Tactics 9
   Team and Group Tactics 13

7. **Defensive Plays and Group Tactics** 31
   Individual Tactics 31
   Team and Group Tactics 46

8. **Offensive Drills** 69
   Ball Handling 69
   Dribbling 71
   Passing 74
   Juggling 78
   Trapping 81
   Receiving 83

Shooting 84

Heading 89

Faking 91

Get Away's 93

Throw-Ins 95

Running 96

Free Kicks 97

9. Defensive Drills 99

Marking (Covering) 100

Blocking 100

Tackling 101

Goalkeeping 104

Sweepers 106

10 Reference Section 107

Offensive Ball Handling Moves 108-112

Introduction

Intent

Many youth coaches have asked me about easily identified offensive and defensive plays and drills they can use. This book is intended to be a supplemental book to my "Teach'n Soccer" book. It is oriented more towards team coaches on youth teams rather than parents at home teaching fundamentals. We will break this down into what they are doing at the time and what plays or tactics to use that will accomplish your goals. My suggestion is use the time you have each weak to maximize what you want to teach. For little kids it's better to break practice drills down into more than one small group to keep everyone busy.

Training Sessions

Then generally keep your group training to around 15-20 minute sessions, blow your whistle, and rotate the kids from one group to the next group. In other words always keep all your kids busy doing something at all times except for water breaks. Don't have any kids just standing around waiting. You get more teaching in this way, the kids don't get bored, and they learn more this way. Get as many assistant coaches as they will let you have, then explain to them what you want each one to teach at their group station. Tell your staff to learn all the kids **NAMES** the first day if possible. Time wise plan your whole practice session. The kids will then learn more in the short periods of time you have for teaching each week. As for the teaching methods we suggest using the "IDEA" slogan approach. *I*ntroduce, *D*emonstrate, *E*xplain what you are teaching, and *A*ttend to all the players in the group.

The Opponent

It's probably smart to try and understand what the teams you play against are doing against you offensively and defensively. Especially after you have played them once you should have a good idea who their best forwards and defenders are. Keep a small pad of paper in your pocket and take notes. Then what you want to do for a game plan is pick the offensive or defensive strategies that will attack, counter, and defeat, what they are doing. Have a game plan before you go into a game, and make sure all your coaches and kids know what it is. Also have a back up plan in case you need it.

Drills

I am going to refer to the drills as "Skill Training Activities" because that's what they really are. Also I am going to throw in a term now being used a lot. It is called "Core Training". What it does is train their body to make certain moves that will make them a better Soccer player. Skill activities will be organized by *"numbers"* so that your assistant coaches can use them and become more familiar with them that way. This way you are all on the same page.

Plays and Tactics

For easy reference the plays and tactics will be organized by *"numbers"* also. They will be arranged as Offensive and Defensive plays or tactics. The legend page will show you the symbols for player movement, dribbled balls, passed balls, tackling, blocking, rolled or thrown balls and kicked balls. Each play or tactic will have a short explanation for how it is supposed to work, strong points, and what it is designed to accomplish.

Strategies

The first strategy I recommend is "have a game plan" to match the team you are playing. Remember though these are only kids, so coach accordingly with your strategies. You know the old "KISS" (Keep-It-Simple-Stupid) phrase. Here are some very basic strategies you can use:

For Offense

1. If you have a team of young players that are not too good at dribbling the ball, have them do more passing and distributing the ball at first until they get better. Have them use the triangle formation method of positioning as they move forward up the field.

2. If you have a good dribbling team, space out your best dribbling attackers so that you have fast speedy runners out ahead of them. This is especially important if you have only one or two good scoring players on your team. Make sure your players understand to spread out and not bunch up in the same area.
3. Have hand signals in place so that your players know exactly what you want them to do in each different situations.
4. Generally speaking have your players with the ball go to the outside wing areas, then when the goalkeeper moves to that edge or side of the goal you pass to a forward or striker breaking to the middle of the field for a quick kick or header for a score.

For Defense

1. Use your better players in goal and teach them well. They will probably stop more shots and at least keep the score close. Your opponent has to score to win games. This is especially important if your team is not too good at scoring.
2. Make sure your players know to quickly get to the player they are supposed to cover (marking). As the play gets closer to the goal, teach them to cover more tightly. And make sure they know who they are supposed to cover.
3. Teach your players to aggressively fore-check regardless of which half of the field the play is on.
4. Near the end of the game if you are ahead, teach them to play for time by disrupting the opponents rush up the field to attack. If necessary even get to the ball and kick it beyond the opponents goal line. This takes up time to get the ball into play again.
5. Make sure your defenders watch the middle of the field for centering the ball by your opponent's for a kick on goal. Also teach your goalkeeper to always glance and check the middle of the field for breaking players.

This way they won't get caught way over at the edge of the goal on a center kick.

    6. Show your players the technique of how to fall back into two lines of defense. Then have your forwards pressure the ball carrier.

Legend for Diagrams

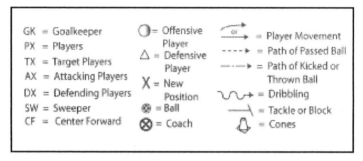

GK = Goalkeeper	◯ = Offensive Player	⌒or→ = Player Movement		
PX = Players	△ = Defensive Player	----→ = Path of Passed Ball		
TX = Target Players				
AX = Attacking Players	X = New Position	—··—··→ = Path of Kicked or Thrown Ball		
DX = Defending Players		∿↦ = Dribbling		
SW = Sweeper	⊗ = Ball	—∖ = Tackle or Block		
CF = Center Forward	⊗ = Coach	⌂ = Cones		

Offensive Plays & Group Tactics

There are a number of offensive plays and group tactics your players need to know. These are plays and tactics they need to know and execute when they are on offense. They break down into "Individual" and "Team or Group" tactics. The individual tactics are coordinated offensive actions a player needs to preform to manage different game situations within the group. We will illustrate the individual tactics first so that you can see how they fit into the group tactics.

Simple Basic Individual Tactics

Receiving and Moving with the Ball (No.1)

Receiving and driving with the ball should always start out with a fake before you take control. The first thing you need to teach your players is to know their own position, know their team mates position and the position of nearby opponent's. The fake is to get to a free open space. Explain to them that in receiving they need to keep their body between the opponent and the ball. To be

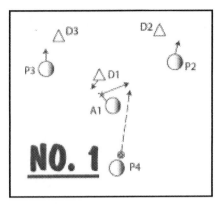

able to do this, make sure your players can control the ball with both feet.

Passing the Ball (No.2)

Play down the field depends on good passing. Passes can be high, low, hard, soft, and with or without spin. Minimal pre leg swing keeps from giving away the direction of the pass. Teach your players how to accurately pass the ball, and without giving away it's direction.

The timing, flight of the ball, and direction are not determined by the player making the pass, but by the player who is receiving it. Teach your players how to read the movements of

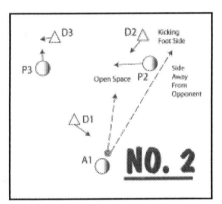

their team mates so that they know where and when to make the pass. Also teach them to have a variety of pass combinations. Some short, some long, some right to a team mate and some to an open space where the receiver can get to it.

Weather also plays a part. In mud or snow, it is best to make the pass high and wide. If the grass is wet, make short direct passes. Teach your players to direct their passes to side that is away from the opponent. And if the pass is going to a forward for a shot on goal, have them direct it to the players kicking foot side.

Flank Kicking (NO.3)

Flank passes are passes that go high over the head of the receiver. If you have a young beginning team though I am not recommending you use this tactic to often. This is because this type of pass, when made blindly, ends up many times right in front of the opponent's goal where they recover to ball. It is a valid pass that can be used with caution. Many times this pass is kicked with spin, which spins away to the outside of the field where a streaking forward receives it for a shot on goal. With practice it can be a very effective tactic.

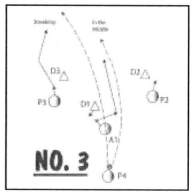

Corner kicks in the form of a flank pass can be kicked with spin toward or away from the goal. Many times this really fools and mixes up a goalkeeper. Also shifts in game action to the middle of the field can be accomplished with a flank pass.

Shots on Goal Short or Long (NO.4)

Shots on goal is a needed tactic because if you don't shoot you don't score. And that means if the opponent's scores just once, they could win 1-0. Shots on goal from long distances are exiting, but not likely to score in a real game. Most scoring is made from short distances.

Shots can be made with the instep, the outside of the instep, with the tip, inside tip of the foot, or the heel of the foot. The success of a shot depends on the accuracy of a kick and not how hard it is kicked. Tactically speaking we recommend teaching your players to shoot from up to about 35 feet (11 meters) away if possible. Teach your players to make their shots as direct as possible, and aimed into the corners of the goal. Have them aim to a spot close beside the goal post, and not at the goalkeeper.

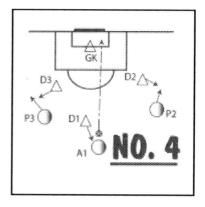

Shots farther away than 35 feet should be aimed directly to the right or left half of the goal, and kicked quickly, sharply and very powerfully. Teach your players to aim at a spot between the goalkeeper and the goal post.

Usually goalkeepers have a weak side, and that is to their left, which is to your right. Tell your players to shoot quickly and suddenly when they are within range. No big leg swing to give away their intension or direction. Any shots on goal from a short distance should direct at the goal. No short passes to a team mate first, should be made.

Tell your players that when they take any shots on goal after dribbling, they should be preceded by faking the timing and direction of the kick. When their kick is hidden it has a much better chance of going in. One way they can do this is kick right off the dribble while turning. This is before stopping their dribble. This is because the goalkeeper won't be able to see them set up to make the kick, or the direction they are aiming at. Also if they kick with their weak foot, it will sometimes fool the goalkeeper.

Teach your players that all shots on goal from a narrow side line angle to the goal should be low and with some spin. And it should be aimed at the far away corner. If the goalkeeper comes out relatively far in front of the goal, they can fake them out by hooking their kick instead of a straight at their target spot kick.

Explain to them that if the grass is wet, "low passes" and "bouncing balls" are hard for receivers and the goalkeeper to calculate what the ball is going to do. So they need act accordingly on these.

Dribbling to Keep Ball Possession (NO.5)

Teach them to keep possession of the ball when they do not have a receiver to pass to because their receivers are all covered

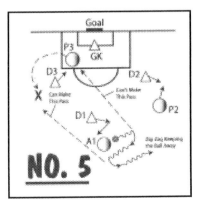

or too far away. Also explain to them that if their intended receiver is in an "offside" position they have to keep dribbling and maintain possession until the receiver is out of the "offside" position.

Show them how to keep possession by dribbling, with no purpose except to keep the ball in midfield, or even better yet in

12

the opponent's half of the field. This tactic can relieve some of the pressure on your team while trying to set up a shot on goal.

Breaking Through Dribbling (NO.6)

Break through dribbling is a way to counterattack from midfield or from open space into the opponent's territory. From what I have seen though most the younger beginning team kids are not good enough yet at dribbling to be able to do this. It is also a good countering tactic to the opponent's "offside" trap play.

Break through dribbling can also be used to take a risk on dribbling in the opponent's penalty area in order to tempt one of the opponent's players to commit a foul. Then if they do you can get a penalty kick which can be a chance to score.

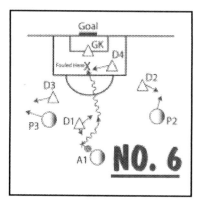

Teach your players to start dribbling from a running position, and not from a stopped position. And to repeat it, always start dribbling with a fake. Also teach them that if at all possible they should always observe their nearest opponent while dribbling, instead of only looking down at the ball or the ground ahead. A lot of dribbling practice without looking at the ball can cure this habit. This is part of "core training".

Simple Basic Team & Group Tactics

Control of the Ball at the Kickoff (NO.7)

In European championships about 25 percent of the goals came from a standard situation play. These goals were from free kicks, corner kicks or penalty kicks. Standard situations depend on two things, the tactics used by the player in possession of the ball or the tactics of the defending team. The offensive team needs to control the ball at the kickoff. Tell your players that they have the advantage because they have the ball. The back pass, then over to the side of the field and up the sideline is the standard way most

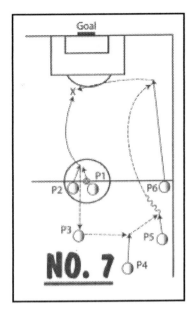

teams use. Notice how the ball is kicked back to the first player (P3), who then passes over to a player (P4) moving up from in back. The player moving up (P4) passes over to a player coming up the side line from in back (P5).

P5 dribbles a short way, then hook passes to a player coming up the side line towards the corner (P6). P6 coming up the side line immediately center passes over to the player (P2) coming up in the middle of the field. From this point the player in possession of the ball (P2) sets up your play for a shot on goal.

Kickoff Quick Counterattack Centering (No.8)

Here is a quick play that sometimes works right after your opponents have scored. In this case the idea is to make a quick kick on goal score while the opponent's are still exited after their goal, and they are not always paying real close attention to what's going on. The ball is driven towards the goal with quick through passes. The back pass control play is not used here. On this play teach your

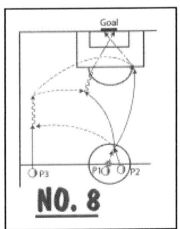

players to get into the open spaces before the defense can get set up.

Here is how it works. The ball is first kicked by P1 to a forward P2 in the circle. The P2 forward immediately makes a flank kick to a forward P3 over toward the side line, who has sprinted out . The forward P3 then tempo dribbles the ball up the side line. After P2 has made the flank kick, they sprint up field to an open space lined up just to one side of

14

the goal. P3 then passes them the ball. They dribble the ball straight ahead almost up the edge of the penalty box, then make a quick kick on goal aiming for the opposite corner.

The alternative play is if while dribbling P3 notices that P2 is covered, they can make a long flank kick to P1 who has sprinted up to a spot on the opposite edge of the penalty box. They then make the kick on goal from their position to the opposite corner, or whichever corner is open.

Kickoff Quick Look In Pass (No.9)

Here is a simple quick play for the little kids to use. It should not be too hard to teach them this play. It's an attacking play. The thought is that if you keep the ball down in the opponents end, they are less likely to score. First P1 makes a short pass to P2. At the same time P4 sprints across in front of P2. which screens out what P2 is going to do. Just after P4 runs by as a decoy, P2 passes to P3

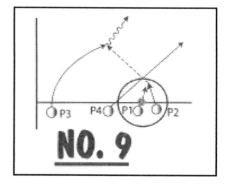

who has sprinted over towards the center of the field just in front of the defenders. This gets the ball in play going towards the opponents goal. P3 then dribbles towards the goal and looks for a pass to a team mate. From here you go to your scoring set up. You can run this play from the other side also to confuse the defense.

Kickoff Standard Back Pass Start (No. 10)

Here is a simple safer play for the little kids to use. It should not be too hard to teach them this play either. It's a slower developing attacking play

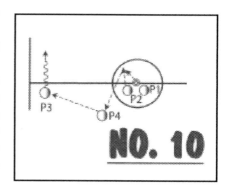

that starts from a back pass to a midfielder (P4), then out to a forward P3. P1 rolls the ball forward to P2, who has quickly moved out in front of them. P2 quickly passes it back to P4, who passes it forward out to a wing forward P3. P3 dribbles the ball forward putting it in play, then looks for a team mate to pass to. From here you go to your scoring set up. You can run this play from the other side also to confuse the defense. Mix it up.

Kickoff Fast Start Back Pass (No.11)

This play is almost like Play No.10, but with a slight variation. This play is safer and gets the ball up field a little quicker than Play

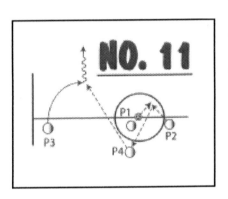

No.10. Instead of the pass going back then over, it goes back and quickly up field to wing forward P3. P1 starts by rolling the ball forward to P2, who has quickly moved out in front of them. P2 quickly passes it back to P4, who passes it forward up field to a wing forward P3. P3 dribbles the ball forward putting it in play, then looks for a team mate to pass to. From here you go to your scoring set up. You can run this play from the other side also to confuse the defense. Mix it up.

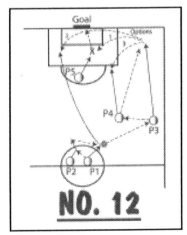

Crossing & Finishing After Kickoff (No.12)

This play is decoying the opposition over towards the side line, then making a crossing pass to center the ball. P1 gets the ball from a center pass back, then passes to P3, who has sprinted up to the middle of the sideline. P3 then passes to P4, who has moved back towards them. After passing,

16

P1 makes a sprint run towards the far side post. P4 then makes an advanced pass ahead of a sprinting P3. When P3 reaches the ball near the corner they make a cross pass in front of the goal. They have 3 options. No.1 they can pass to P5 in front of the goal. No.2 they can pass to P1 at the far post. No. 3 they can pass to P4, who has moved to the corner edge of the penalty area. You can run this play from the other side also to confuse the defense. Mix it up.

Attacking Shadow Play (No.13)

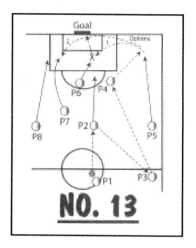

This play is also decoying the opposition over towards the corner, then making a crossing pass to center the ball. I call this the zig zag effect. It can get the defenders confused, especially the little kids. P1 gets the ball around midfield. They pass it to P2 in the center of the field. P2 passes it back to P3 at midfield. P3 passes the ball to the feet of P4. P4 passes the ball just ahead of a streaking P5 running towards the corner. P5 makes a crossing pass to center the ball.

They have 2 options. No.1 they can pass to P6 in front of the goal. No.2 they can pass to P7 coming up near the far post. P7 and P8 make attacking runs toward the far post in case they can get a rebound or deflection shot on goal. You can run this play from the other side also to confuse the defense. Mix it up.

Overlaps and Crossing Runs Play (No.14)

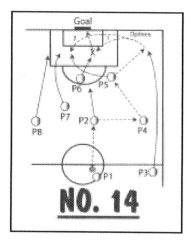

This play is also decoying the opposition over towards the corner, then making a crossing pass to center the ball. I call this the zig zag effect play also. It can get the defenders confused, especially the little kids. P1 gets the ball around midfield. They pass it to P2 in the center of the field. P2 passes it over to P4 at midfield. P4 passes the ball to the feet of P5. P5 passes the ball just ahead of a streaking P3 running towards the corner. P5 then runs behind P6 and attacks the back post. P6 attacks the near side post. P3 makes a crossing pass to center the ball.

They have a number of options. No.1 they can pass to P6 in front of the near post, No.2 they can pass to P5 coming up near the back far post, or they can pass to P7 making an attacking run at the back far side post. P8 also makes an attacking run toward the far post in case they can get a rebound or deflection shot on goal. You can run this play from the other side also to confuse the defense. Mix it up.

The Long Corner Kick (No.15)

Corner kicks always have to take into account the weather, field condition, how good is the opposition, how good is your corner

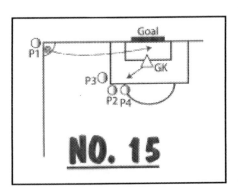

kicker and how many of your players are in the goal area. Since this is a long kick, your kicker has to be good at making long straight or flank kicks (spinning). If your kicker is very good, you can use this play.

First teach your players in the goal area to bunch up more over on the near side edge of the penalty box to bring the goalkeeper out towards them, thinking you are going to use one of them to head the ball into the goal. This leaves room for your corner kicker to flank kick or spin kick the ball in order to get it to curve into the goal.

Head Level Kick to the Inside Corner Kick (No.16)

How this kick works is your corner kicker kicks the ball inside right to the lower edge of the "goal area" at head height.

Player P2 runs to a predetermined spot at the edge of the goal area, when the kick gets to them they either do a backwards header into the goal or they let the ball hit them, roll down to their feet, then they can just kick it in.

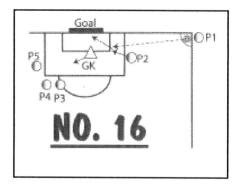

I would only use this play occasionally as a quick surprise play. It might just work with a young team where the defenders don't catch onto what you are doing. And if the players bunch up at the far side edge of the penalty area, and act like the ball is going to come to them for a header or kick in, then the goalkeeper might get fooled and be out of place.

Short Corner Kick (No.17)

How this kick works is your corner kicker kicks the ball to player P2 who is only a short distance away. P2 gets the kick and dribbles quickly into the penalty area. What you have to be careful of on this play is that the opponent's don't trick your players into an offside trap. Make sure you teach them how to NOT get tricked into the trap.

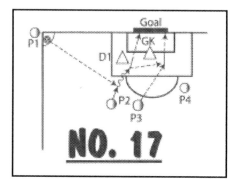

When P2 gets in position to make a kick on goal, they can make the kick or they can pass to a team mate P3, who is not off side. This play is a little safer for a young team because you usually keep control of the ball. This is also a good play for you to use if you have a strong decisive dribbler on your team to act as P1. P4 can act as a decoy.

The Back Pass Corner Kick (No.18)

How this kick works is your corner kicker kicks the ball to P2 who comes toward them from the end line corner of the penalty

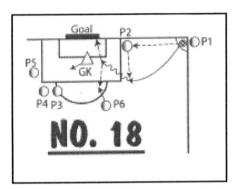

box. The corner kicker P1 then sprints in towards the outer corner of the penalty box. P2 then makes a quick pass right back to P1 sprinting in. P1 then dribbles the ball in towards the goal box and takes a shot on goal if it's open. If it's not open they can pass it back to P2, or they can look for a team

mate (P6) outside of the penalty box to pass to. This is usually a fairly safe play for a young team because your team keeps the possession in most cases.

The Standard Center the Ball Corner Kick (No.19)

How this kick works is your corner kicker makes a high flank type kick aimed right in front of the goal near the edge of the

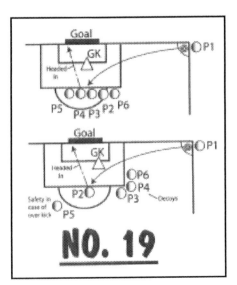

penalty box. This could be a straight kick or a curved spinning kick. It depends on what your best kicker can do best. There are several ways you can set this up. One, you can have a group of your players right out in front of the goal.

The idea being whoever the kick comes down to in the group, heads it into the goal. Two, you can have one or two of your best headers right in front of the goal. Your other players are spread out to the sides as decoys. The idea here being there will be more of a chance that the ball will come to your best header, and they will head it in.

The other players try to decoy the defenders away so that your best header has the best chance to get to the ball. There is another variation that you can try. Instead have your corner kicker loop the kick to P6 who tries to head the ball over the head of the goalkeeper. Either way this play is probably going to work best for older more talented teams, not the real little kids. This is because the younger teams probably don't have a kicker that can make the kick, or a header that can get to the ball and head it in. Make sure you teach your kids to all look first and see where the goalkeeper and defenders are all located. This is very important in order for this play to work. If your players can learn to decoy and trick the goalkeeper and close defenders away from right in front of the goal, the play will have a better chance of working.

One other thing to mention here. As soon as the ball is kicked your players can charge in towards the goal from outside of the penalty box line. Just have them make sure they don't get caught on an off side trap. As long as one defender and the goalkeeper are between them and the goal they are OK. Teach and show them how to time their charge into the penalty box area while the kick is in the air. Hopefully it drops right in front of them where they can choose to kick it in or head it in.

The other thing you need to do is have right footed kicking players charging in if the kick is from the right corner, and left footed kicking players if the kick is from the left corner. This gives them a better chance of making a quick kick as soon as it drops if they can't get under it to make a header.

The Standard Direct Free Kick (No.20)
The idea on a free kick is set up and make the kick as quickly as possible before the defense can set up. So teach your players to hustle on this play. How this kick works is your best kicker makes the kick. What he does is going to depend on where the referee places the ball. First make sure all your players understand that the opponent's must be at least 10 yards away.

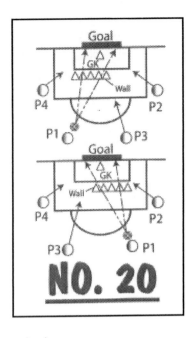

NO. 20

Usually the opponents set up a wall of players to block the kick. The best chance against the wall is to kick the ball over their heads, then teach all your players to charge in for a rebound or deflection. Where your kicker aims is going to depend on where the goalkeeper is standing. Make sure they check quickly where the goalkeeper is.

If he is standing in the middle they can aim for either corner. Also if there is room they can try to spin kick a curve shot around the wall. Practice all of these possibilities so that your players all learn to quickly asses the situation, then make the shot that has the best chance of going in.

If your kicker is kicking from the left side, and the goalkeeper moves to the left corner of the goal, have them aim for the right side corner. If he moves over to the right side corner, have them aim for the left side corner. If the ball does not go in and there is a rebound or deflection, make sure all your other players charging in have glanced to see which side the goalkeeper is on. Then if they get the ball have them aim for the opposite corner from where the goalkeeper is located.

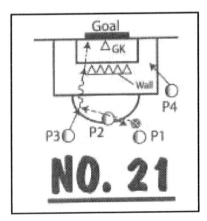

NO. 21

The Indirect First Touch Dribble In Free Kick (No.21)

The idea on this indirect free kick is on the first touch the attacker dribbles around the wall and shoots. This is a trick play because P2 runs towards your kicker P1 who kicks the ball between the legs of P2 and over to P3 who is charging in. P3 then dribbles around the wall and spin kicks the ball into the goal with their left foot if possible.

Why do want to teach them to spin kick the ball in. This is because the ball curves and makes it very difficult for the goalkeeper to judge what it is going to do. If the goalkeeper can't block or catch the ball, and it rebounds or deflects, P3 follows the shot, keeps charging in, and tries to kick in the rebound. This may be a hard play for the little kids to learn, but if they can learn how to do it, then it becomes a good weapon in your offensive arsenal. Sometimes you need a trick play to level the field.

The Indirect Second Touch Dribble In Free Kick (No.22)

The idea on this indirect free kick is to get a crossing pattern misdirection going to confuse your opponents. How it works is P1 kicks the ball over to P2 going to the right. P2 then passes the back the other way to P3 who is charging in. P3 takes the pass, dribbles around the wall and spin kicks the ball in using the left foot if possible. P4 needs to act like they are going to get a pass to decoy the goalkeeper over to the right side, which gives P3 a better chance to get the ball into the left corner of the goal.

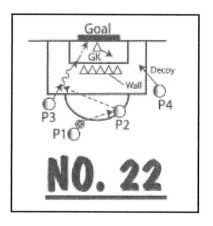

The reason for the spin kick is it's harder for the goalkeeper to determine where the ball is going, and many times it rebounds or deflects off the goalkeeper. This offers a chance for another kick if P3 follows their shot in. Also sometimes the kick deflects or rebounds off the other way to the right. If this happens it gives P4 a chance to charge in behind the wall and kick it into the goal. This is another tricky play that will level the playing field so to speak if you can teach it to the younger little kids.

The Indirect Deflect Left Second Touch Free Kick (No.23)

The idea on this indirect free kick is to make a fake pass to a player P2 right in front of the wall, who then deflects it right back to a player P3 charging in. How it works is P1 pretends to pass it to P2 trying to make the defense

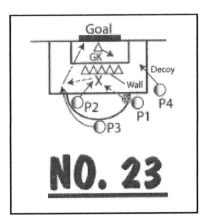

think they are going to turn and dribble around the wall for a shot on goal. What P2 actually does is sprint to a spot right in front of the wall, turn, then immediately deflect the pass back to P3 who is charging in towards the left side of the wall. P4 charges in toward the right side hoping to fool the goalkeeper into thinking the pass may go to them. If the goalkeeper bites on the decoy, and moves to the right side of the goal, it gives P3 a better chance of kicking the ball into the left corner of the goal.

The Indirect Deflect Right Second Touch Free Kick (No.24)

The idea on this indirect free kick is to make a fake pass to a player P2 right in front of the wall, who then deflects the ball to

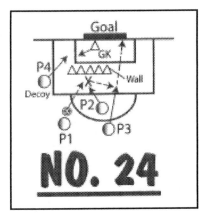

P3 coming around in back. P3 then quickly makes the kick into the right corner of the goal. P4 charges in toward the left side hoping to fool the goalkeeper into thinking the pass may go to them. If the goalkeeper bites on the decoy, and moves to the left side of the goal, it gives P3 a better chance of kicking the ball into the right corner of the goal.

Penalty Kick Alignment Play (No.25)

The idea on this kick is to make a goal because you basically have a free kick. Remember the offside rule is in effect during the penalty kick. Make sure your players all under stand what offside means. There are probably several approaches to the best tactical alignment. Because this book is more for the younger beginning kids, I am going to keep it simple. First make sure your best goal kicker takes the kick.

He is the key to this play working. It's not as easy as it may look, but you can practice and teach kids to make this play work. Make sure all your players understand that the ball is live as soon as P1 makes the kick. At that point they can charge the goal. Also make sure they understand they can get no closer to the ball than 10 yards, and they have to be outside of the penalty area. And by the way, the penalty arc is 10 yards away from the ball spot

Here is what you have to teach your penalty kicker to do. Depending on the age, they may be able to kind of decoy or look at the right corner of the goal when in fact they want to kick it into the left corner of the goal. So what they do is kick it real hard just to the left of the goal keeper. And if you can teach them to do it, have them spin kick it. This way it may deflect or rebound off the goalkeeper. Then P2 or P3 charging the goal has a chance to score.

Throw In From Deep in Your Own Territory (No.26)

When you are making a midfield throw in from deep down in your own territory, have your sweeper (P10) or deepest defender get free, come up, and take the throw. This is when an opponent D2 is attacking. P10 then dribbles the ball forward down the field and immediately look for a team mate to pass the ball to. Then return to their sweeper position.

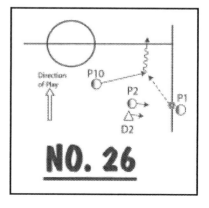

Throw-in In Front of the Opponent's Goal Area (No.27)

When you are making a midfield throw in towards the goal area, and there is a defender (D1) coming up to mark your throw in player, then have them throw

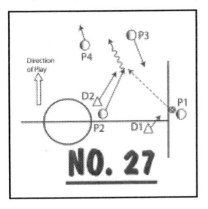

the ball in just a little ahead of the player P2 into free open space. Remember you work in three's. So P3 comes back in towards P1 so that if the ball gets away from P2 they are right there to receive it. P4 who was up the field a bit moves towards the penalty area. This play will work from the opposite side of the field also.

Throw In Midfield With Opponent Defending (No.28)

When you are making a midfield throw in and there is a defender marking your throw in player, then have them throw to an

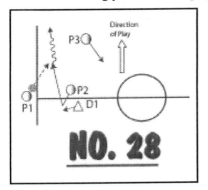

open space going forward. P2 fakes going one way then comes back, receives the ball and dribbles down the sideline. Remember you work in three's. So P3 from in back moves into free space. P1 comes back in bounds and moves behind P2 down the sideline. This play will work from the opposite side of the field also.

Throw In Midfield After Opponent Was Attacking (No.29)

When you are making a midfield throw in after recovering the ball, have P1 pretend to throw the ball forward to P2 and P3, then throw the ball in back way over the head of P2 into free space. P2 and P3 act as decoys for receiving the throw in. Have your Sweeper or deepest defender get free by running in the direction of the ball. When they get the ball, turn and look up field for a team mate in the clear, then pass them the ball. After that they return to their sweeper position. If P2 and P3 do a good job of acting, they should decoy the opponent's in the other direction in order to keep the ball safe in your end of the field. This play

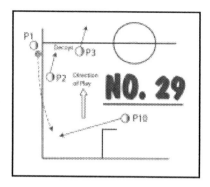

will work from the opposite side of the field also.

Throw-in In the Corner near Your Goal (No.30)

This is a slightly different play or tactic designed to help you score a goal when you are in a tight corner. The idea is to get a corner kick or another throw in chance. The corner kick will probably

give you a better chance to get a shot on goal. As you can see the goal is pretty well blocked. This will be the case most of the time in this situation. Here is what P2 needs to do.

They can get a corner kick by kicking the ball against defender D1, and having it deflect off. This is sometimes referred to as achieving a secondary target (D1). If the ball does accidentally deflect the other way, then P3 should

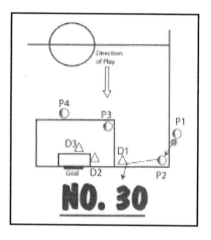

be ready to come to it and make a kick on goal. This tactic is not used too much, but it could work for you.

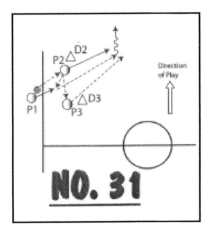

Throw-in Up, Back and Forward (No.31)

This is a pretty common play or tactic that is pretty easy to teach little kids. Basically P1 throws the ball in forward to a player P2, who is well marked by a defender. The receiving player then drop passes the ball back to P1 or another support player like P3, who then plays ball forward to another team mate moving towards the goal.

Throw-in Trick Play Anywhere on Field (No.32)

This is a trick play you can use when you want to get the ball down the field quickly, but no team mate is in a position to

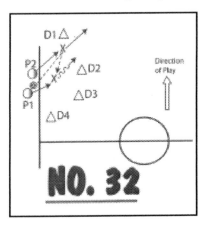

receive it. Two of your players, P1 and P2, stand very close to the ball out of bounds. P2 picks the ball up as if to throw it in, but then they drop it and P1 picks it up instead. P2 then runs onto the field with their back to P1. As soon as P2 gets a few yards into the field, P1 throws the ball very hard against the back of P2. Hard enough that it bounces right back to P1, who starts to dribble or pass the ball up field. This play can work if you are willing to practice it with your players.

Triangle and Diamond Passing to Move Up field (No.33)

Here is where working on short passes in groups of three come in to play again. Also split, or connect in a diamond pattern of short passing, helps your team move up the field. By moving up field this way it creates small groups that are capable of keeping

28

the ball away from defenders. It also draws in defenders to create space up field. Here is how it works. Group 1, 2, 3 and 4 move forward down the field short passing the ball to their support team mates within their group and the other groups *SEE DIAGRAM 33*.

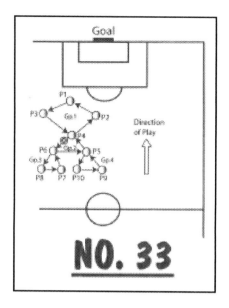

As an example within a group such as Group 2 (3) if P4 becomes challenged, they move the ball around over to P6 *SEE DIAGRAM 33-A*. If the defender D4 attacks deeper, P6 passes the ball around to P5 and on around back to P4, who is open to move forward *SEE DIAGRAM 33-B*.

If everyone in their group is challenged at the same time, they pass the ball over to group 3 or 4. If they are not challenged, they can pass the ball up to group 1 in a diamond pattern as they move forward. It's probably a good idea to identify your groups with some kind of hand signal because if you see something they don't, then you can signal them what

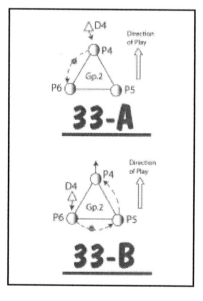

you want that particular group to do. Practice your groups of three together so that they get used to working with each other.

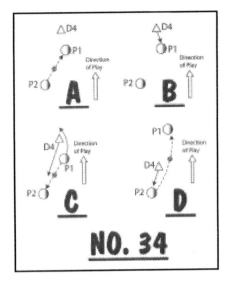

Triangle Group or Individual Short-Short-Long Play (No.34)

This type of offensive strategy play can be within a group, or from group to group. How it works is P2 passes the ball forward to P1 when at all possible *(SEE DIAGRAM 34-A)*. D4 defender attacks and challenges P1 *(SEE DIAGRAM 34-B)*. P1 immediately drops the ball back to P2. Defender D4 pursues the ball back to P2. P1 then moves forward to open space *(SEE DIAGRAM 34-C)*. P2 then makes a long pass to P1, who has moved to open space moving forward. D4 gets decoyed out of position, opening up forward open space *(SEE DIAGRAM 34-D)*. This type of play is usually used down the sideline where it works best because your players are shielded by the sideline on one side from attack.

Give and Go Play (No.35)

This is one of the oldest and maybe best two player up field play in Soccer. It is sometimes referred to as a "wall pass". This

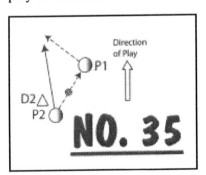

play works really well if you can get the defender D2 to pause even for just a few seconds. The key to this play working is speed and quickness.

The second P2 makes the pass (the Give) to P1, they break straight ahead sprinting right past D2. This is a one touch pass right off the foot (the Go) of P1 to a spot just ahead of the sprinting P2. If you practice this play with all your players often, it will work.

Defensive Plays & Group Tactics

There are also a number of defensive plays and group tactics your players need to know. These are plays and tactics they need to know and execute when they are on defense. They break down into "Individual" and "Team or Group" tactics. The individual tactics are coordinated defensive actions a player needs to preform to manage different game situations within the group. We will illustrate the individual tactics first so that you can see how they fit into the group tactics.

Simple Basic Individual Tactics

Kickoff Defensive Intercept Play (No.36)

This type of defensive strategy play is designed to intercept the opponent's back pass. Here is how it works. Center forwards, D1 and D2, one on each edge of the center circle, are positioned to attack P3. The second that the kickoff player P1 kicks the ball forward to P2, these two players charge the player P3 that usually gets the back pass to start the opponent's play.

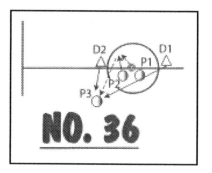

This may not work every time, but with little kids it may work until they catch on to what you are doing at the kickoff. Have a signal to your players for when you want them to do this.

Corner Kicks Protecting the Goal (NO.37)

This is individual players protecting the goal on corner kicks. You have two players D1 and D2 stand on each side of the goal post when there is a corner kick. One protects the near post, the other the far post. They can't use their hands like the goalkeeper, but they can use their head or body to deflect the ball. The goalkeeper (GK) is basically in the middle. Make sure they understand they

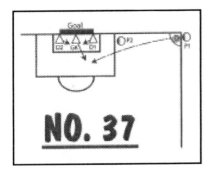

have to stay near the post itself, and not obstruct the goalkeepers view. If the goalkeeper has to leave the goal area box to protect the flanks, then each player moves to the middle of the goal area to protect both halves.

Corner Kicks-Protecting Front of the Goal Area Box (NO.38)

This is individual players protecting the front of the goal against kicks and headers on corner kicks. You basically have three players

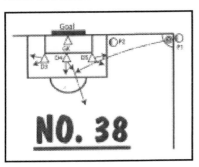

D3, D4, D5 stand right on the front edge of the goal area box. Most scoring will be from short kicks or headers. What each player has to do is be ready to kick or head the ball down the field if they can get to it.

Make sure they understand that they can't touch it with their hands, but they receive on the chest, let it drop in front of them and kick it away. Or if they are in the right position, they can direct one touch kick it clear down the field. Make sure you know who the opponent's best headers are. When you see them or very tall kids move in front of the goal. Give a signal for your team to be ready for a header in front of the goal.

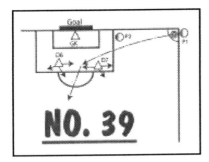

Corner Kicks-Protecting Front of the Penalty Area Box (NO.39)

This is individual players protecting the front of the penalty area box against kicks and headers on corner kicks. You basically have two players D6, and D7 standing in the front part of the penalty box. Their job is to protect against headers, short kicks, or long kicks that are taken in front of the goal and penalty box area. They clear them out as quickly as possible to prevent a goal.

Corner Kicks-Protecting Against short Kicks (NO.40)

This is one special individual player protecting the area 10 yards away from the corner against short kicks and medium kicks on a corner kick. You basically have P8 guarding against a short kick to P2, a drop pass back to P1, or a medium kick to P3 out on the near corner of the penalty box. Basically this is a 1 on 2 situation. So this player has to be very smart not to get decoyed out of position on any fake kicks.

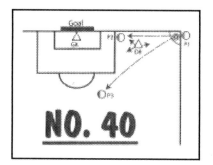

Corner Kicks-Constructing an Offside Trap (NO.41)

This is a special two individual player action to quickly set up an offside trap. If the opponent's are not paying attention they can get caught in this trap. How this works is if the ball has been kicked out of the penalty area to the feet of an opponent (P3) instead of in front of the goal, then this player has to be attacked immediately by two players such as D9 and D10 simultaneously.

The second D8, and the rest of the team near the goal can see the kick is going out to P3 instead of in front of the goal, they all very quickly sprint down

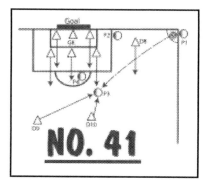

the field. If your opponent's are not paying attention this can leave P2 and P4 in an offside position. This can happen with young teams. This gives you a chance for an indirect free kick scoring opportunity.

One-on-One Coverage (NO.42)

This is when a defender concentrates on one particular player. They can either cover them closely (pressing cover) or lightly (6-10

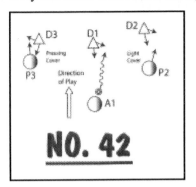

feet away). Pressing cover can mean body contact. It is more difficult for the offensive player to lose a defender when there is just a small space between them.

Basically a defender in a cover (marking) situation should be in a position that will place them in between the opponent and their own goal. Teach them to keep their eyes on the opponent and the ball (continued glancing). Teach them to stand on the side that is closer to the ball, diagonally ahead of the advancing opponent.

Coverage In Between Space (NO.43)

An individual player takes over space coverage only when

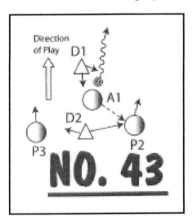

a team mate is outnumbered. The player, in this case D2, positions themselves between two opponents and keeps their eyes on both. The defender D1, who is closest to the ball and the goal, must only cover the opponent lightly. If the ball is passed to one of the two opponents P2 or P3, the one who is the likely receiver is attacked immediately with one-on-one coverage.

Sweeper Individual Tactics (NO.44)

The Sweeper is the "free man" in the defense. Because of his position on the field he has a better view of how the game is developing. So he kind of becomes the captain, director, or QB of the defense. They can guide the movements and actions of their team mates. A sweeper can do many things for you out on the field, so it's probably a good idea to have one. Pick several of your smart and savvy kids to be the sweeper, and start training them young. In the long run you may be glad you did.

When the ball carrier starts to get close to the goal the sweeper starts to move with the ball. If a team is trying to gain possession from a one-on-one, the sweeper moves up behind them to provide cover. The distance between keeps narrowing as the opponent approaches the goal *(SEE FIGURE 44-A)*. When they get close tell them to be no more than 6-10 feet behind their team mate.

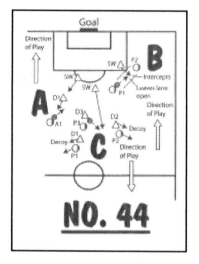

When the play gets up close to the goal then the sweeper, who does not have a particular player to cover, works on safeguarding open space and lanes. Teach them to decoy a passing lane, then at just the right time break in between and intercept the ball *(SEE FIGURE 44-B)*.

Also teach them to come up from near the goal area and join the offense on counterattacks. Usually no player covers them so that they are free to come up, take the ball, and move it up the field without much opposition from the opponents *(SEE FIGURE 44-C)*. When D1, D2, D3 see that they are tightly covered, they look for the sweeper to "give and go" with. They can make room for this play to work by decoying P1, P2 and P3.

Goalkeeper Individual Tactics (NO.45)

What They Need to Know

The Goalkeeper has much different strategies and tactics from the other players. The real big difference is they can use their hands and touch the ball. I believe this is the most important position on the team. If you have a well trained goalkeeper, your team will always be in the game because the score will be close. Don't fall

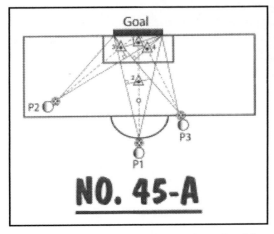

into the trap that so many young beginner coaches do. They think they have to let every boy or girl on the team experience every position. So what happens is your goalkeeping is only fair at best. This is because no player is there long enough to learn the position like they should.

My advice is take anywhere from 2 to 4 player that are quick and smart, then teach them the position. Make sure you get some adult to work with your goalkeepers all the time, and teach them all that they need to know. This is proven to work over and over again. You will win more games, your team will be better, and the kids will have more fun. Isn't that what it's about.

Here are the things you have to teach them:

- Where to position themselves in the box and in front of the goal.
- Their basic position during shots on goal.
- How to catch or punch the ball.
- How to handle the ball from a dribbling forward.
- How to build a "wall" against a free kick.
- How to handle the "penalty kick".
- How to handle the offensive action.
- How to handle the defensive action.

Working in the goal area box

Here is what they need to work on to position themselves in the box. Basically it depends on where the shooter is. That tells them when to move out in front of the goal, or move back right in the goal (*SEE FIGURE 45-A*). The best position to be in is in the center of the angle from the shooter to both goal corners. When you look at *FIGURE 45-A* and trace the lines, you begin to see how being in the center gives the goalkeeper and equal distance each way to block, catch, or punch the ball. Also notice that when they come out in front of the goal area box, they have less distance to each side to stop the shot.

Free kick situations

Situations like free kicks and corner kicks are particularly difficult for goalkeepers, especially when the penalty box area is crowded. You have to teach them to make quick split second decisions. The only way to help them learn is to set up all the different kick situations, then explain what they have to do in each particular situation. Sometimes, mostly with the little kids, you will have to do "walk through" until they catch on.

Distance away from goal to play

There are some general or basic RULES as to what distance from the goal that the goalkeeper should play. Basically it depends on how far the ball is from the goal:

- If the ball is in the opponent's half of the field, they step out to the front edge of the penalty box and line up to where the ball is coming from to catch through balls. This is really important when you are playing with only 3 or 4 defensive players and no sweeper.
- If the ball is in their half of the field up to about 25 yards in front of the goal, they stay on the front line edge of the goal area box. This is so that they are not surprised by wide passes or dropping air balls that are curving and spinning.
- If a break away opponent approaches all alone with the ball and reaches the penalty area, the goalkeeper runs towards them in a way that will shorten their attack angle.

Body position

Here is another basic RULE to teach them. No matter where they are when they stop, have them shift their weight forward onto the balls of their feet and be ready for action with their arms spread (stance). From this position they can act quickly. Tell them never lean backward.

Incoming Ball's Flight Path

The angle of the ball's flight path and the direction from which the opponent is approaching the goal is also important. Here are the rules to follow. 1) As the opponent approaches and the space in which they can make their shot is a 45 degree angle, tell your goalkeeper to take the position as shown in *FIGURE 45-A*. 2) If the opponent approaches at a sharp angle, tell your goalkeeper to move back towards the goal at an angle of about 23 degrees (about half of 45 degrees). From this angle they can control balls that are kicked spinning and curving into the long or far corner. This angle also works for incoming flank opponents and back passes.

Position of Team Mates

Teach them to learn to be aware of the positions of their own defensive team mates around the goal. They can do this by quick glances, then focusing on the ball. Here are more basic RULES they need to learn. 1) As long as a team mate is engaged in a "one-on-one" situation with the ball carrier, have them remain in their normal position right in front of the goal. 2) If a team mate is covering part of the goal, you can have them move more towards the unprotected area which gives them better odds at stopping the shot. Just be sure that the team mate understands they can't use their hands, only their head and body to block the shot.

Punching and Catching Ball's

Catching and Punching basic RULES. 1) Teach your goalkeeper that incoming balls which they feel they can handle should be caught and not deflected away. 2) When the ground or the ball is wet, or when they are not sure they can catch it, have them punch it away. 3) Because the reach to catch balls is long when using the two hands technique, then if the ball is out at an extended reach have them punch the ball away. 4) Any balls that are kicked into the penalty area from the right side should be punched away from the penalty area to the left side using their right hand, and just opposite from the other side.

Now when I say punch the ball, it does not mean you only have them use their fist. They can learn to use the palm or flat part of their hand to do the punching also. This lets you teach them to do several things. This lets them easily push a high ball over the top horizontal goal bar behind them, or a low ball away around the corner of the goal post.

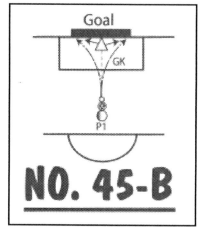

Penalty Kick Situations

Teach your goalkeeper that as soon as they hear the referee's whistle for a penalty kick, they need to get into their tactical location quickly. This is so that they don't get caught out of position. To trick the kicker teach them to get ready, but act and look very confident. In older groups this sometimes impresses and psyches out the kicker. If you are coaching an older group, and you have played the opponent's before, you may want to keep a book on their kickers so that your goalkeeper knows their tendencies. Many times they always kick to the same spot, in spite of faking. Knowing that will give your goalkeeper the edge.

For the shot itself, teach your goalkeeper to focus and concentrate on the ball and the kicker's foot. This takes away from being faked by head, eye, and upper body moves. This gives them the information they need. The foot swing gives away which corner they are aiming for. Have them get a lot of practice for this by having the other goalkeeper take turns with them at making shots at both corners. This is how they learn "muscle memory" reactions *(SEE FIGURE 45-B)*.

Once they get into position they can also make lots arm waves back and forth, and upper body leans of their own to try and fool the kicker. Statistics have shown that goalkeepers who anticipate the corner of the shot, then leap or move in that direction just seconds before the actual kick is made, have the best chance to block it. It's all in the timing though from lots of practice. Goalkeepers committing too early on the kickers run up will give them a chance to adjust their angle at the last minute.

Leaping for the Ball

Usually good goalkeepers don't have to leap if they get in the right position for the kick. If they do have to leap, here is how to

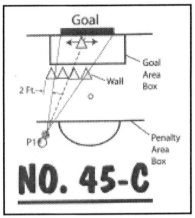

teach them. To make a leap to the right they begin by crossing the left leg in front over the right pivot leg in the direction of the leap. Next move is a step with the right leg to start the jump. To go to left is just the opposite.

Positioning a Free Kick Wall

A well positioned wall can stop a free kick. There are several opinions as to who should position the wall. Most older division goalkeepers usually want to position the wall themselves. The other opinion wants to give the authority to a defensive player who can stand immediately behind the ball and signal the wall players where to move to line them up in the most advantageous position. One of the problems with the goalkeeper doing the alignment is they have to leave the center area of the box to see how to make the alignment. When they do, they can get caught out of position if the kicker makes a quick kick.

When your goalkeeper positions the wall they should call each players name calmly, but in a loud, clear and distinct voice. Basically the wall is positioned out 2 feet beyond the direct line between the ball and the goal post *(SEE FIGURE 45-C)*. When the free kick is taken inside of the goal area box, make sure your players know they can set up the wall right in front and on the goal line even if the ball is less than 10 yards away.

Timing of Free Kicks

The timing of free kicks is very quick. When there is a free kick foul the referee blows a whistle, then raises their hand for indirect free kicks. Next they fairly quickly place the ball on the ground at the spot of the foul. Before the free kick can be taken the ball has to down on the ground though. Then the opponent's have to wait at least 2 seconds after the whistle and the ball has been placed before they can make the kick. At the sound of the whistle all defending players have to try and get at east 10 yards away from the ball. So what you have to teach your players is back up going away from the ball and in line with the goal.

Then if the kicker tries to make a sneaky quick kick before the defense can set up, and the kick hits your player trying to move away and the ball deflects away, then it's a legal block. But instruct your players that they have to at least be trying to move away the 10 yards even if they don't make it. After the goalkeeper catches the ball they have 6 seconds to clear it out. And the opposition can't obstruct them from getting rid of the ball in time. The key is when your players are on defense near their goal area box or penalty box area, explain to them that they have to get back very quickly to set up the wall or protect the goal from a quick kick.

Goal Kicks

If the attacking team kicks the ball accidentally over the goal line, then it's a free goal kick. And many times it's the goalkeeper that makes this kick because they are usually one of the better kickers handling the ball in the dangerous goal area box. The idea is to kick the ball clear, and way out away from your goal area. The ball can be placed anywhere on the 6 yard goal area box line.

But for safety reasons it's usually placed out on either corner as far away from your goal as possible *(SEE FIGURE 45-D)*. Make sure your kicker understands that to get clear, the ball has to go past the 18 yard line (penalty box line) without touching anyone. One way to do this if there are opponent's in front of them, kick an air ball or flank kick instead of on the ground.

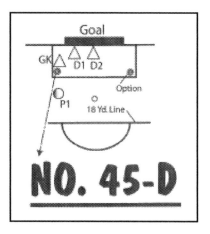

Goalkeeper as Chief of Defense

Since the goalkeeper is a key player on the team, usually a smart athlete, in a better position to see the whole field, you can teach them to direct the defense. Teach them to pay attention to the game. Also this keeps little kids from being bored back at the goal waiting for the play to come back in their area. From their position they can see the gaps in the opponent's defensive coverage of their team mates.

Here is how to teach them to do this. Call out loud the team mates name, followed by a one word instruction. As an example, "Billy-Left". This would be telling Billy to move, dribble, or cover to their left. When you are practicing have your goal keeper coach spend some time back with your goalkeeper, explaining and showing them how to do this during play. This is how they learn.

Goalkeeper and Offense

As part of the transition from defense to offense the goalkeeper has an important function. After they make a save they can start the counterattack by getting good deep passes out to a team mate in their half of the field. Teach them how to make the different types of passes. If the team mate is not too far away, they can just roll the ball out to them on the ground (*SEE FIGURE 45-E*).

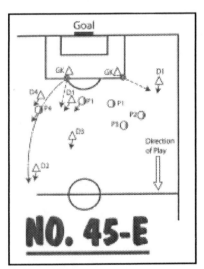

NO. 45-E

Long air ball passes can be difficult for the real little kids to handle. Show them how to make longer air ball passes though for the older kids who can handle them better. The whole idea is get the ball out quickly to your attacking forwards up field.

If most of the opponent's are up near your goal, that means there is open space at midfield. So a quick accurate outlet pass really gives your team a great chance for a break away goal at the

42

other end. The more you keep the opponent's out of your end of the field, the less chance they have of scoring.

Outside and Inside Defender Individual Tactics (NO.46)

It's probably going to depend mostly on your teams basic defensive strategy, tactics, and formation. But basically your "outside" defenders will cover their direct opponent near the side line. Try to recover the ball if possible and back up the sweeper on keeping the opponent to the outside of the field, instead of letting them move to the center of the field for a shot on goal, or a pass for a shot on goal *(SEE FIGURE 46-A)*.

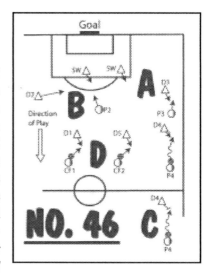

If the ball is being played on the opposite side of the field from them, they move towards the goal to help the sweeper cover open space in front of the goal *(SEE FIGURE 46-B)*. As long as the ball is down in the opponent's side of the field, they can use the slide tackle to intercept the ball from a dribbler. This way if they miss they can still get up, recover and chase the ball carrier *(SEE FIGURE 46-C)*.

Basically your inside defenders attack the opponent's center forwards in the middle of the field *(SEE FIGURE 46-D)*. It is so important that the inside defenders stay in the middle. They should NOT get too involved with the offense on counter attacks, or take over other defensive tasks. Basically teach them to stay in the middle of the field and hold their positions. This way if the opposition recovers the ball on a steal, then mounts a quick counterattack they don't get caught way down in the other end of the field.

When defenders do get involved with the offense (basically outside) and go on the attack, they should finish their attack fairly quickly with a positive action. This would usually be either a flank pass or a long shot on goal.

Midfielder's Individual Tactics (NO.47)

Every midfielder has defensive tasks. They are responsible for being able to switch very quickly from offense to defense. They

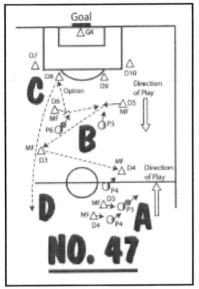

also have to try and shift action from one side of the field to the other. Sort of corral and force the opponent to move towards the other side of the field. This is to disrupt the opponent's game rhythm, tempo and flow (*SEE FIGURE 47-A*).

Good teams that play with four or more Midfielder's often pair them up together. If you do have 2 pairs of Midfielder's, have only one pair at a time get involved with the offense at transition time.

When your Midfielder's are counterattacking during transitions, teach them to move the ball diagonally back and forth across the field (*SEE FIGURE 47-B*). This accomplishes several things. One, it confuse the opponent's sweeper if they have one. Two, it wears down the opponent's so that they are slowed down a little in the second half of the game.

From these positions out on the wing they use flank and back passes to their own back line of defense (*SEE FIGURE 47-C*). Sort of like "keep away". This will really mess up an energetic attacking type of team. Then with long passes from their back line (*SEE FIGURE 47-D*), they will force a defensive orientated team to go on an offensive attack prematurely.

Center Forward's Individual Tactics (NO.48)

Some teams use center forwards to really confuse a young or inexperienced team. They will cross and change places right in front of the lead attackers, or in front of the goal as they move around in combination play (*SEE FIGURE 48-A*).

Basically they are out in front of the defense and look for the opponent's to make a mistake in their own territory. If they can get control of the ball, they just try to move around and maintain control until their Midfielder's can move up and help *(SEE FIGURE 48-A)*.

Or they can move in the direction of the sweeper which ties up the sweeper and a defender. This tactic clears up open space for Midfielder's to move up into, and mount an

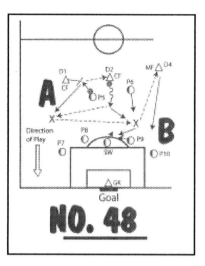

attack *(SEE FIGURE 48-B)*. If you are going to use center forwards (CF) make sure you pick 4 kids who are fast, and they can control the ball with either foot. If you have the little kids, teach them how to do this. There are advantages in using center forwards. If they can gain control of the ball they can use the following four tactics to really confuse a young inexperienced team.

1) they can keep changing position from right to left, and left to right while using combination play *(SEE FIGURE 48-A)*. 2) One player can start to move at an angle towards the rear, then the other player will move forward at an angle so that the team mate with the ball has the opportunity to pass either wide or short *(SEE FIGURE 48-C)*.

3) In front of the goal in a small space, one dribbling player can drop pass the ball over to a team mate next to them while decoying an attacking opponent away *(SEE FIGURE 48-D)*. 4) To get ready for "flank" passes, both center forwards D1 and D2 run diagonally across the field,

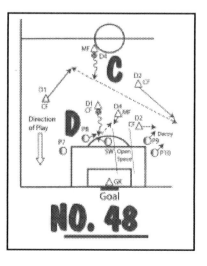

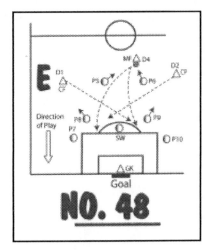

NO. 48

passing each other as they head for one of the goal posts. The short passes are handled by the player on the short side while the long passes are handled by the other player *(SEE FIGURE 48-E)*.

Simple Basic Team & Group Tactics

The following is more for young beginning coaches. Basically Soccer is a defensive game. These are general team teaching TIPS and RULES.

- Always stay on the goal side of attacking opponents, between them and the goal they are attacking.
- Tell them that if they been assigned a specific player to mark (guard), stick with their mark wherever they go.
- Always try to delay attacking players so that they can't run quickly past your defense and score an easy goal.
- Tell them to always keep their feet moving, and be ready to shift position to guard an attacking player.
- Teach them to play off the opponent a yard or two, and wait for the best opportunity to steal the ball.
- Tell them to always take responsibility for their area of the field.
- Teach them to study and understand their position and it's importance to the rest of the team.
- Teach them that when they are in doubt as to what to do, then clear the ball out of bounds, down field, or anywhere away from the goal area.

If you can teach young kids the RULES right from an early age, they will do fine playing soccer. What I see happening though is kids grouping up around the ball (herding) or running all over the field. You have to start young with them or they will learn bad habits.

Team strategies and tactics start with basic formations (full field 10 on 10). Then to allow them more touches on the ball you can play some small sided games in practice, like 3 on 3, 5 on 5 and 6 on 6.

Through this section we will occasionally refer to players with specific names that apply to their special positions and tasks:

GK= Goalkeeper SW= Sweeper CF= Center Forward
MF= Midfielder DB= Defensive Back FB= Fullback
HB= Halfback CHB= Center Halfback LF= Left Forward
RF= Right forward F= Forward WF= Wing Forward
RH= Right Halfback   LH= Left Halfback S= Striker
CHB= Center Halfback MS= Middle Striker ST= Stopper
OM = Offensive Midfielder

Basic 4-4-2 Formation (NO.49)

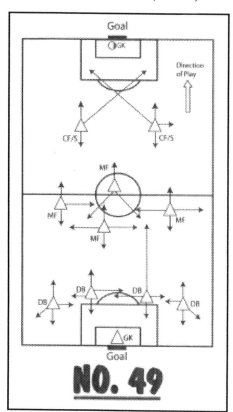

This is about as basic as you get. It is flexible though. I am going to show the most common alignment and slight variations.

The four does not mean they have to be in a straight line. What it means is there are 4 DB's and 4 MF's. The arrows indicate the general area they cover.

The German and European teams will use this alignment a lot.

The reason I like the way this particular alignment is set up is because there is less open space in between the players than if they are in a straight line across.

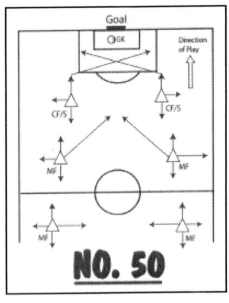

Variation 4-2-2-2 Formation (NO.50)

This is just a variation of the 4-4-2 formation. Basically two of the Midfielder's move up right behind the forwards. You might use this alignment shift when the opposition has lots of players or loads up right in front of the goal. Because this means your forwards need help. The bottom four are the same as in the regular 4-4-2, with the same tasks.

You can develop a signal when you want them to shift into this formation. This formation does have some merit because you can attack better up the middle. This will work really good if you can decoy some of the opposition out to the wings.

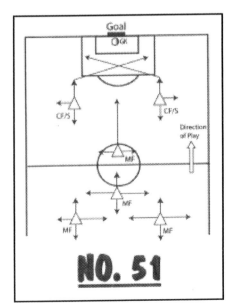

Variation 4-2-1-1-2 Formation (NO.51)

This is just another variation of the 4-4-2 formation. Basically one of the midfielders moves up to the bottom edge of the center circle. The two outside midfielders come down and in a little. The bottom four are the same as in the regular 4-4-2, with the same tasks.

The front midfielder stays almost in the same spot as in the regular 4-4-2 alignment. This alignment might be one to use when the opponent's have been breaking away and attacking straight up the middle of the field. If they get through the front midfielder, then the midfielder right behind them cuts them off. You might use this alignment shift when the opposition loads up, and has lots of players coming down the middle.

Variation 4-4-2 Formation (NO.52)

This is just another variation of the 4-4-2 formation except the bottom four and the midfielders are different.

The midfielders are in the form of an arc, and they rotate in both directions. The bottom four is really a sweeper plus three DB's. The top two forward's are the same as in the regular 4-4-2, and they have the same tasks. This may be a good formation to use if your opponent's are scoring on you around the goal because the sweeper will be there to help your goalkeeper.

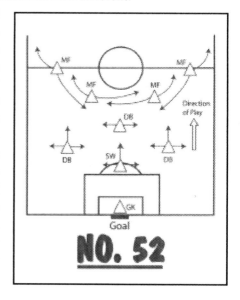

Basic 4-3-3 Formation (NO.53)

This is just a little different from the 4-4-2 formation. It has three DB's and a sweeper (4), three midfielders and three forwards. This formation is used more in high school or college. Many coaches say don't use the formation with a sweeper. They say when you have young kids and put a sweeper in back, they get bored back there waiting, and they don't learn much because they don't get the action.

However, if your opponent's have a good striker, and he is scoring on you all the time then this may be an alternative. So you put this player more up front as a MF, but lets say the score is 6-1

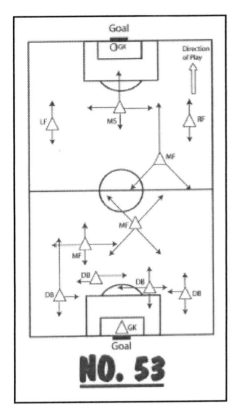

against you because the opponent's are scoring all the time right up the middle. Do you think that same player is learning and having lots of fun up in the middle of the field as a MF? I don't think so!

Sometimes you will have a young player that is big for their age, but not very fast at running up and down the field. Sweeper might be a good place for them. Start teaching them the game and what to look for. Tell them how important a sweeper is, and my guess is they won't miss all that running up and down the field.

This is a pretty common formation for high schools and colleges. It is also balanced well for attacking or defending. So it might be a good formation to start a young team on, rather than let them run aimlessly all over the field chasing the ball. This formation may also work with your groups of three's tactics, going from midfielders to forwards. This variation alignment appears to be favored by the European teams. The arrows show the areas each player generally defends.

Variation 1-2-1-3-3 Formation (NO.54)
This is just a little different from the regular 4-3-3 formation. It still has three forwards, three midfielders and four defenders in back of them. The difference is in the middle and in the back. The midfielders move into a triangle, and the defenders move into a 1-2-1 diamond. The front player in the diamond is a stopper. Their job is to stop the play right when it gets up to them. Then comes two

50

DB's out on the wings. The back player in the group is the sweeper. The forwards play just about the same place as in the regular 4-3-3, they align the same and have the same tasks.

This variation is used a lot in high schools and colleges. This is another good starting formation to use with young kids. It is balanced and pretty easy to understand how it works.

The stopper marks the opponent's forward striker if they have one. Or they follow the center midfielder on the opponent's team. The sweeper just moves back and forth across the field, and follows the ball

Variation 4-3-3 Formation (NO.55)

This is just a little different from the regular 4-3-3 formation. It still has three forwards, three midfielders and four defenders in back of them. The difference is the alignment in the middle and in the back.

The North American

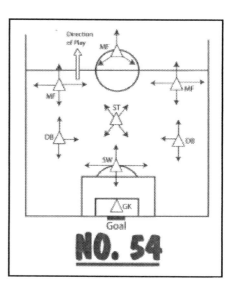

NO. 54

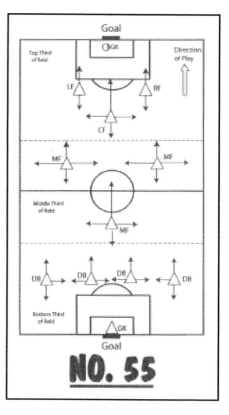

NO. 55

Soccer League teams used this variation a lot back in the 70's. The difference is the middle forward is pulled back towards the midfield, and the center midfielder is dropped back in the middle. This formation has a strong back line of four near the goal. The middle of the field is weak though. This means that if your opponents are any good they will be down in your end of the field a lot. If you do not have a good scoring team, it could be a long day for your team always trying to stop them down in your end of the field.

Basic 4-2-4 Formation (NO.56)

This is a little different defensive formation. It still has four forwards, only two midfielders, and four defenders in back of them.

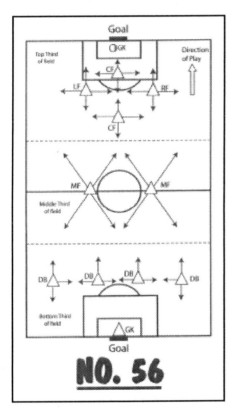

This formation is designed to score when you can recover the ball. It's probably the most offensive minded defensive alignment in modern times.

I'm not sure this formation will work for young teams though. To make it work, you must have talented forwards and midfielders. They have to strike early, and learn to hold the ball for long periods.

When your opponent's have the ball, the pressure is really on your midfielders. If they stop the opponent's attack then the ball will be down in your end of the field a lot. And it could be a long day for you. You could try this with a young team though if you have the talent, skill, and speed to pull it off. And they learn fast.

Basic 3-5-2 Formation (NO.57)

This is a little different defensive formation. It has a strong midfield alignment. Many coaches say today's game is won in the midfield. In other words keep the opponent's bottled up in the middle of the field, and out of the scoring area. If you have a young team this may work for you if your team is not to good at scoring.

At least the opponent may not score as much. A 0-1 or 0-2 loss may be much easier for your players to handle if they are not to good. If your midfield is not operating efficiently though you won't have much ball possession or scoring opportunities. The key here shut them down in the middle of the field with lots of bodies.

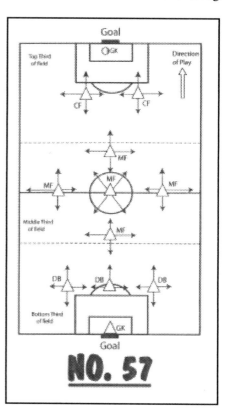

Variation 3-5-2 Formation (NO.58)

This is a little different defensive alignment for this formation. The German's seem to like this variation. They make one of the DB's a sweeper and drop them back a little. Then they move two of the midfielders up to the right and left of the "middle half of the field". The other three midfielders drop down to the bottom of the "middle half of the field". They even make it harder to get into the outside parts of the "middle half of the field". This is a tough defense to break.

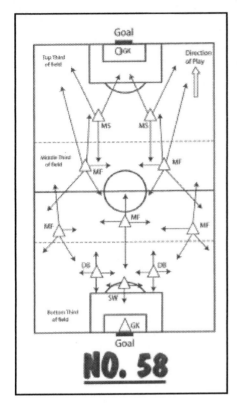

Goal

NO. 58

The five midfielder's have the midfield all bottled up, then if they do break through your sweeper is there to guard the open space in the rear to stop them. This could work for a young team that has trouble scoring, and want's to hold the opponent's scoring chances down so that they can keep the game close.

Also with the large number of players in the middle of the field it is easier to use today's more modern team tactics like fore-checking and pressing. This makes it more fun for the younger kids to try different new defensive techniques. I can see this might work for a young team if you spend the time to teach them the techniques and skills they need to make this formation work.

Basic 3-6-1 Formation (NO.59)

This is a little different defensive formation. It has one of the strongest midfield alignments. Many coaches say today's game is won in the midfield. In other words keep the opponent's bottled up in the middle of the field, and out of the scoring area. It does have some problems though. If the opponent's break through, it's weak down near your goal. And with only one forward, it is harder to score up near your goal. I guess it could work for a very young team, but I'm not sure I would like to try it.

Some very good coaches have tried to change to this after using a 4-4-2 defense, and got shut out in two out of three games.

54

I guess what I am saying is if you decide to use this formation then understand what you have to teach to make it work. And make sure you have the players with the skills you need to make it work.

Then stick with it and make it work.

One coach gives some tips on using this formation. If your team is trailing and trying to tie up the match, take out one of your forward midfielders for a forward up front. If your team is leading, then replacing a midfielder in the rear with a defender, or replacing a forward up front with a midfielder, are

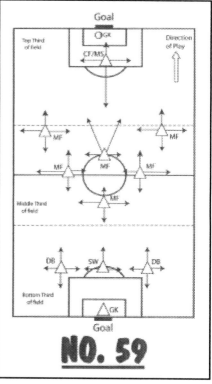

tactical moves that will work for you. Many German teams like to use this formation as a tough away game tactic just to gain a 0-0 tie instead of a loss.

Basic 4-5-1 Formation (NO.60)

This is a little different defensive formation. It has one of the strongest midfield alignments. Many coaches say today's game is won in the midfield. In other words keep the opponent's bottled up in the middle of the field, and out of the scoring area. It is similar to the 3-6-1 formation, except it is stronger down near your goal because a midfielder is replaced by a defender down in the rear of the formation. German teams like to use this formation a lot when they are playing a team that they feel is stronger than they are.

It does have a big disadvantage though because your forward striker is almost always marked by two defenders. This makes it very difficult to score by passing them the ball. About all

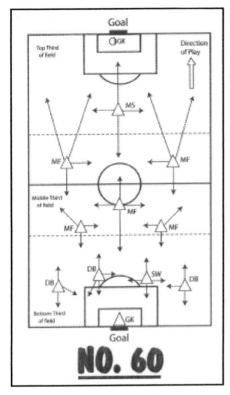

you can expect to do using this formation is get a tie unless you have a very talented team and a really great play to get the ball to your forward striker.

As in the 3-6-1 formation if you decide to use this tactic then make sure you understand how to make it work, then teach it to your team and stick with it. If you have a young team and not much talent and skills to score yet, then you might use this to go for a 0-0 tie instead of losing most of your games. Just a thought. Loses are not fun for your team, trust me on this.

Basic Flat Back Four 4-6-0 Formation (NO.61)

This is definitely a little different defensive formation. It appears to be a spin off from the 4-4-2, but with a very different alignment. Basically it has four defenders and six midfielders. Many coaches say today's game is won in the midfield. In other words keep the opponent's bottled up in the middle of the field, and out of the scoring area. This formation does that. Plus it replaces the two forwards of the 4-4-2 formation with midfielders, and places one along each sideline. Their job is to run the entire sideline and cover the outside portion of the field defensively. This allows the flatback four to stay compact in the middle of the field to shut down offensive attacks by your opponent's.

The single offensive midfielder (OM) in the middle checks back to the defense if the defense can recover the ball. Then receives the ball offensively as the point man. They then draw the opposing teams defense to them so that they can create space for the three midfielders who become forwards and move ahead at transition.

The flat back four position themselves out about 30 yards from the goal so that they can execute offside traps when on defense. The goalkeeper plays a sweeper/ keeper position, and aggressively comes out of the goal to challenge through balls.

I really like this formation. You might be able to use this with a young youth team if you have the talent and skilled players, especially for the

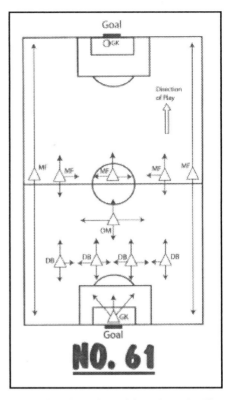

five midfielders. You will need to do a lot of teaching though. The two outside midfielders will have to have a lot of running endurance, and the middle three will have to be able to change to aggressive forwards on offense.

Basic Flat Back Four Group Tactics (NO.62)

This is the strategy and tactics for your flat back four defenders as a group. If the opponent's striker or forward breaks through and makes a run down the right side of the field, the right outside and inside defenders (DB's) move over and immediately get an angle on them. Then they double team the opponent's until they give up the ball or the DB's recover the ball. The inside left defender (DB) will move over to a position at least about 3 yards behind and 5-10 yards to the left of them as a third line of defense.

They also watch for runs in from the midfield, then move to the ball if the striker breaks through somehow. The outside left DB

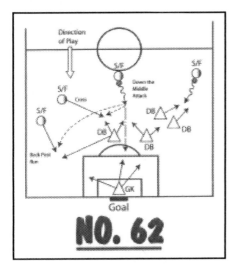

NO. 62

moves over and waits at about the center of the field to break up any cross runs, and marks any opponent that makes a run at the back side post. If an opponent makes a run down the left side of the field, it work in reverse or flip flopped.

If a striker or forward makes a run right down the middle of the field, then whatever ball is being passed to them should go right at the goalkeeper, or they will get quickly and aggressively separated from the ball by the two middle DB's. If you are using a flat back four in your formation make sure you train them well, over and over on these tactics.

Basic Defending Formation Just at the Kickoff (NO.63)

This is a very basic formation for a defense just at the kickoff. Teach all your defenders that they have to remain outside

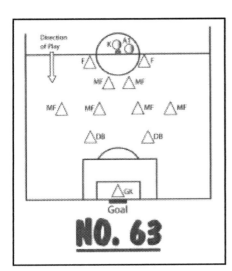

NO. 63

of the center circle until the ball is touched. At that moment they can use any number of tactics or strategies. When the whistle blows the kicker must move the ball forward.

So what the kicking team usually does to get the ball back is make a short forward kick pass to a team mate right next to them, who has made a few quick steps forward

58

towards the ball. They then quickly drop pass the ball back to the kicker or another team mate, to start play.

So you can start with the alignment shown here which is pretty common, then have two midfielder players charge or attack the player getting the drop back pass *(SEE PLAY NO.36)* and try to get a steal, or you can have your players immediately drop back into the defensive formation you want them in for your overall defense. Basically this defending formation is more of an attacking the opponent's offense at the kickoff tactic, than it is a prevent defensive alignment.

Small Sided Game Tactics (NO.64)

Small sided games are for the little kids and youth teams, and they vary all over the country. The idea is don't overwhelm 5 or 6 year olds with playing or practicing in a 10 on 10 with a goalkeeper type game situation. What happens is you have games from 3 on 3 to 7 on 7, and everything in between. So as the coach, what do you do?

It's going to depend on how many players your team has, and what their age is. And that seems to vary all over the country from league to league. Some coaches use a goalkeeper and some don't. What they do is use one or two cones for a simulated goal or as a target to get a score. What you are going to have is defenders, midfielders and forwards. Each one of your players needs to learn what to do at each of these positions. You can rotate the beginners around so that they learn each position.

The idea is let each little kid get lots of touches and have fun. This is how they experiment and learn how to control a soccer ball in more of a game type situation. Before you play any of theses games with your team though make sure they have been through at least some of the skill training drills. Because if you don't, it's going to be just "herd ball." These little kids need at least some idea of the skill they need to be using out there. What I am going to do is attempt to show at least one diagram for each game, to give you some ideas. I'm not going to show them all because there are just too many possibilities. To simplify it, I will be using the recommendations of the "US Youth Soccer" manual for small sided games. As an example No.64-3 will be for the 3 on 3 game, and so on.

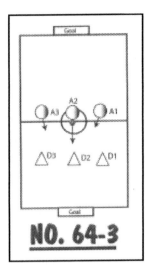

NO. 64-3

3 vs 3 Game

I'm going to start with the 3 on 3 game. This is basically designed for 4 and 5 year olds (U6). Each side will have three players and no goalkeeper. Recommended roster size is 4-6 players. Play everyone on your roster, with each player getting at least 50% of the total playing time. At this level the players can be coed (boys & girls). If you are using both halves of a regular field, your roster size can go up to 8.

Field size is 20-30 Yds. long, 15-25 Yds. wide, with a 4 Yd. Diameter center circle. Goals are 18 Ft. wide with a 6 Ft. high cross bar, but may be smaller. If you don't have a goal though use cones. Or you can even make goals by gluing PVC pipe fittings together.

The ball is size 3. Use unrestricted substitution at any stoppage. Use FREE PLAY for these real little guys, no positioning. Encourage all players to dribble and pass, but don't force them. I know it's going to be "herd ball" at first, but do the best you can. The game will have (4) equal (8) minute quarters, with a two minute break between quarters. Have a half time period of 5 minutes while you talk to them. You can use one mom or dad, or an assistant coach for the referee. Make sure all fouls are briefly explained. All fouls result in a direct free kick, with all players at least 4 yards away from the ball.

Use corner kicks at the corners, goal kicks from at least 2 or 3 yards away from the goal, and all players at least 4 yards away from the ball. Use the regular type soccer rules for most everything else. Don't use any red or yellow cards. They wear all the same type equipment, everything. On throw-ins though put the ball flat on the ground, and have them kick it in with the side of their foot. And don't count the goals, just let them play and have fun.

4 vs 4 Game

This is basically designed for 6 and 7 year olds (U8). Each side will have four players, and a goalkeeper is optional. Play everyone on your roster, with each player getting at least 50% of the total playing time. Field size is 25-35 Yds. long, 20-30 Yds. wide, with a 4 Yd. Diameter center circle. Goals are 18 Ft. wide with a 6 Ft. high cross bar, but may be smaller if necessary. If you don't have a goal though use cones. Or you can even make goals by gluing PVC pipe fittings together.

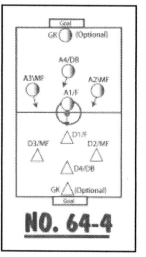

Basically all the rules are the same as 3 vs 3. However if you want to play exactly to the letter of the rules, go to "US Youth Soccer" and print out a copy of the small sided game manual. The big difference is it's 4 vs 4. "US Youth Soccer" is recommending no goalkeeper, and the ball size is still No.3. Recommended roster size is 6-8 players. And NO offsides is called.

Play everyone on your roster, with each player getting at least 50% of the total playing time. If you are using both halves of a regular field (dual field), your roster size can go up to 10 or 12 for each field. The game is divided into (4) equal (12) minute quarters. Same rest periods between as in 3 vs 3. I would think at this level you may want to break into boys teams and girls teams as long as you have enough players to do that.

It's at this level that they recommend you start teaching the connections to the full game. Start by pairing up the players. Now here is where it gets tricky. Some experts are saying use a 2-2 alignment while others say use a 1-2-1 diamond. From all the accounts I have read I am favoring the 1-2-1 alignment. By pairs I mean start to teach working together back and forth to move the ball.

Teach each player the three general passing directions of soccer, forward, backward and sideways. Introduce positional play. One defensive back (DB), two midfielders (MF) and one forward (F). All the major components of team play are represented this way. Show each player what their visual cues are, and what their decision making should be at their position.

Rotate players every quarter, or as necessary so that each one gets time at each of the three positions. I have coached this age

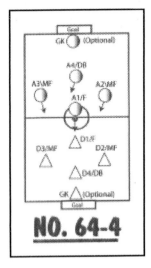

NO. 64-4

group many times. They are more capable of understanding than you think, at least most of them. So don't hold back on explaining, but ask them question to be sure they understand.

Basically still just let them play, but if "herd ball" starts to take over too much, then have an agreement to call time out and get back to the basics. If you use a goalkeeper as many leagues do, designate a coach to stay back and work with the goalkeepers while play is going on at the other end of the field. At this level have them roll the ball out like in bowling. I see soo many kids in goal at this age that have no idea what to do back there.

If you don't do this they never learn. I see so many teams where there is no coach or anyone back explaining to these young kids what to do. Whoever you get to do it, make sure they teach the kids ALL the skills and moves. Another fair rule is when you DO NOT use goalkeepers at this level, then explain to your players that the ball must travel below knee height when there is a shot on goal for scoring. Also MAKE SURE spectator and team benches are on opposite sides of the field.

5 vs 5 Plus a Goalkeeper Game (6 vs 6)

This is basically designed for 8 and 9 year olds (U10). Each side will have five players and a goalkeeper. Play everyone on your roster, with each player getting at least 50% of the total playing time. Field size is 45-60 Yds. long, 35-45 Yds. wide, with a 8 Yd. Diameter center circle.

Goals are 18 Ft. wide with a 6 Ft. high cross bar, but may be smaller if necessary. The wider the better though. The more goals they score, the more exited they will be about playing soccer. If you don't have a goal though use cones. Or you can even make goals by gluing PVC pipe fittings together, then bury them in the ground.

Basically all the rules are the same as in regular soccer with all the free kicks. No slide tackling allowed though. Throw-ins are regular overhead type throws. However if you want to play exactly to the letter of the rules, go to "US Youth Soccer" and print out a copy of the small sided game manual. The big difference is it's 5 vs 5. "US Youth Soccer" is recommending a goalkeeper, and the ball size is No.4. Recommended roster size is 9-11 players per team. NO offsides is called. And goalkeepers can punt or kick the ball away.

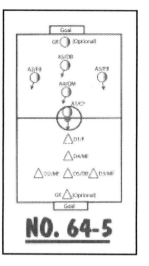

NO. 64-5

Play everyone on your roster, with each player getting at least 50% of the total playing time. If you are using both halves of a regular field (dual field), your roster size can go up to 14 or 16 for each field. The game is divided into (2) equal (25) minute halves. Use a 5 minute rest period between halves. I would think at this level you may want to break into boys teams and girls teams as long as you have enough players to do that.

It's at this level that they recommend you start teaching overlapping, pressure, cover, balance and combination play. As an example combinations of A5-A1-A4 or A5-A4-A2. Teach A2 and A3 to pressure and cover. Teach A4 to help A2, A3 to help A1, and how to receive ball a deep position. Now here is where it gets tricky again. Some experts are saying use a 1-3-1-1 alignment while others say use a 1-1-2-1-1 diamond plus one. From all the accounts I have read I am flavoring the diamond plus one alignment.

There is also a number of ways to distribute the types players like defenders (FB/DB), midfielders (MF) and forwards (CF/F). All the major components of team play are represented this way. Blow a whistle and rotate your players every 5 minutes or so is a good plan. This way they can get some work at all the positions. Remember this is a training game. Show each player what their visual cues are, and what their decision making should be at whatever position they might be playing. Don't just turn them loose out there (herd ball).

8 vs 8 (With a Goalkeeper) Game

This is basically designed for 10 and 11 year olds (U12). Each side will have five players and a goalkeeper. Play everyone on your roster, with each player getting at least 60% of the total playing time. Field size is 70-80 Yds. long, 45-55 Yds. wide, with a 8 Yd. Diameter center circle (almost full size).

Goals are 18 Ft. wide with a 6 Ft. high cross bar, but may be smaller if necessary. The wider the better though. If you don't have a goal though use cones. Or you can even make goals by gluing PVC pipe fittings together, then bury them in the ground. All the goal and penalty areas are marked.

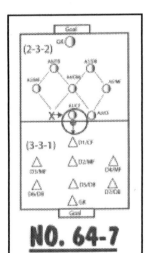

Basically all the rules are the same as in regular soccer with all the free kicks. Except free kicks are awarded the opposing team at the center circle. Players have to stay at least 8 yards away. Penalty mark is at 10 yards instead of 12 yards. However if you want to play exactly to the letter of the rules, go to "US Youth Soccer" and print out a copy of the small sided game manual. The big difference is it's 7 vs 7 on the field.

"US Youth Soccer" is recommending a goalkeeper, and the ball size is No.4. Recommended roster size is 11-13 players per team. And goalkeepers can distribute the ball by punting or kicking the ball away. Play everyone on your roster, with each player getting at least 60% of the total playing time. The game is divided into (2) equal (30) minute halves. Use a 5 minute rest period between halves. At this level you break into boys teams and girls teams.

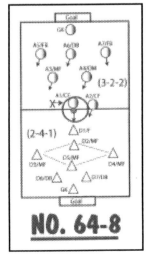

It's at this level that they recommend you start teaching each player to make individual decisions. They need to learn offense and defense and how to transition. Midfield play is introduced at this level. Also train two center backs (FB/DB) to cover and balance. Train two center forwards (F/CF) to combine and score. Train the flank players (MF) how to play in all three thirds of the field. Also make sure all your players understand the "triangle" and "diamond" passing techniques.

Continue to show them overlapping (A6 & A7 around A3 & A5), zonal defending and double teaming. Train D2 to coordinate with D1 & D5. Train D3 & D4 how to operate down the length of the flanks. Now here is where it gets tricky again. There is also a number of ways to distribute the types players like defenders (FB/DB), midfielders (MF) and forwards (CF/F). All the major components of team play are represented this way. Some experts are saying use one of any of four alignments, the 2-3-2 (better for offense), 3-3-1 (better for defense), 3-2-2 (better for defense) and 2-4-1 (better for offense).

Have an arrangement to blow a whistle and rotate or substitute your players every 5 minutes or so is a good plan. This way they can get some work at all the positions. Remember this is a training game. Show each player what their visual cues are, and what their decision making should be at whatever position they might be playing. At this level don't overtrain, but don't just turn them loose out there either (herd ball).

Basic Formation for Corner Kicks (NO.65)

As you go up in levels and divisions, most goals are scored on corner kicks. And more often than not they score on headers. Here is a good defensive formation against corner kicks. For what each player does go back and *SEE PLAYS 37 THROUGH 41*.

D1 and D2 forwards stay out more to midfield so that they can start a counterattack

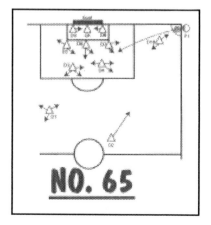

NO. 65

very quickly if their team mates gain possession. This may not work every time, but it's a good start for the little kids.

To pick your kids for each positions, here are some guidelines. D8 and D9 should have skills like the goalkeeper. They also need to be able to jump and move quickly, and without using their hands. D3 through D7 should be also able to jump high and head the ball away from the goal. D10 has to be very quick on their feet and smart. This is because they have to be able to tell where P1 is going to attempt the corner kick.

Basic Alignment for Penalty Kicks (NO.66)

During penalty kicks the offsides rule is in effect. So what

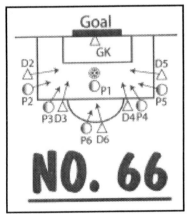

you have to teach your players to do is quickly line up strategically like in the diagram. What each player has to do is jump out in front as soon as the ball is kicked so that they block out their opponent as they go for any deflections or rebounds.

This is similar to blocking or screening out in basketball, except they don't use their hands or bring them up. Tell them they can head the ball away if it's up in the air. If all the offensive players get screened out, the job of the goalkeeper is a little easier. Then he can concentrate on the kicker.

A TIP here. Players are taught to kick to the weak side of the goalkeeper, which is usually the left side for a right handed goalkeeper. The other thing they are basically taught to do is spin the ball and make it deflect off the goalkeepers leg and into the corner of the goal. With this in mind train your defenders to watch for either one of these plays, then be in position to defend against them on any deflections or rebounds.

Basic Tactics for Defense against Throw-Ins (NO.67)

You need to teach your players to notice when the ball goes out of bounds to the opponent's, then quickly look for opponent's

66

nearby that will try to get the throw in from their thrower. Then mark them and try to intercept the ball. First thing is teach them to quickly glance where there is free space nearby where the thrower will aim for. See where they are looking and break to that area for an intercept if they have no one to mark *(SEE NO.67-B)*.

A TIP here. When there is a throw-in down near your half of the field and near to your goal, teach your defenders to be aware of a long hard throw-in to a player right in front of your goal. Explain to your goalkeeper to watch for a player or players breaking towards the goal.

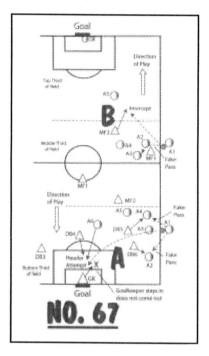

What your goalkeeper needs to be careful of is coming too far out in front of the goal. What some upper level teams like to do is make a long hard throw-in up in the air that comes down to their player who heads it into the corner of the goal *(SEE NO.67-A)*.

If your goalkeeper has the angle they should stay close to the goal and try to grab the ball, or punch it away or over the bar. Another good idea is first either you or your goalkeeper coach sit down with them and explain the different tactics the offense will use on throw-ins. When they learn all of this, they will be better at setting up to stop any scoring directly off the throw-in.

Basic Signaling in Tactics and Strategies (NO.68)

This is one of my fun things to do with little kids. Everybody keeps trying to convince me that you can't do this with little kids. But you know what, I've been doing it for years. Most little kids think it's cool. I tell them that it gives them an edge. First thing you need to do is have offensive and defensive captains out on the field. They relay the play to your other players. And change captains every once in a while. It let them all in on the fun. If you do it right the kids really do have fun with it. Generally I have not had any problems with 6-8 year olds doing this.

Why do you even want to do this? I have watched young teams out on the field where the coach is yelling out instructions from the sideline. Many times I notice the kids don't hear them. The idea with the captain is they have to keep glancing over at you so that they won't miss a signal. That's the key.

There is a whole lot of ways to do this. I'm just going to give you a few so you can get started. Lets say you are behind in the game and you don't want the opponent's to score. You want your defense to fall back closer to their goal and tighten up. You could call out your captains name if they are not looking, then raise one hand, palm up and forward, then slowly bring it back wards like half a wave motion. Or you could hold up one hand high in a fist (meaning tighten up back near your goal in your defensive formation). I know these are kind of "hokey", but kids understand the significance, believe me I've tried it.

Or lets say you are behind and need a goal badly. You could have a signal for a play you have worked on where your forwards and midfielder's attack with overlapping short passes until they get in close and get the ball to your best one or two strikers. One signal could be you raise both hand up in a fist, and then cross them in an "X" (symbolizing overlapping triangles or diamond groups). Especially for the real little kids if the signal relates, and you explain that to them, they catch on real quick. As I say I have tried this, and it works.

Now, when you are working with the older kids you can make more complicated signals. Also if I suspected the opponent's were stealing my signals, one thing I have done is to have several coaches or players send in signals, two being fake, and one being the real signal. I have a lot of fun doing this. It just drives coaches nuts that are trying to cheat by figuring out what I am going to do. You do have to be clever though and not outsmart yourself. I try to follow the term "KISS", **K**eep **I**t **S**imple **S**tupid when at all possible when I'm doing this. The other key is everyone must know what each signal actually means.

Offensive Skill Training Activities (Drills)

All drills will also be numbered for "EASY " reference.

The offensive drills will cover all the types of skills that young kids playing soccer need to know to get started off on the right foot. Some are "Core Training" and most all involve "Muscle Memory" training. What they do is train the body and feet of your kids to make certain moves that will make them a better soccer player. The skill activity drills are numbered so that you can have your assistant coaches use them and become more familiar with them for reference purposes between you, them and the kids.

These drills will cover the very basic fundaments like dribbling, passing, ball control, trapping, receiving, tackling, throwing, heading, kicking, shooting at goals, blocking, faking, juggling, goalkeeping and running. We will also try to cover some special techniques that will help them.

The plan with teaching these drills is stay with small group stations where you or one of your coaches is teaching one of these skills. Keep the time period short, maybe 15 -20 minutes. Then blow a whistle and that group moves to the next station to learn another skill. The size of your groups will depend on how many kids you have on your team, and how many instructors you have.

As an example if you have 20 kids on your team, then you could have 4 groups of 5. And then you would need 4 stations and at least 4 instructors. The bigger your group is though the more problems you will have. Smaller groups mean more touches. If you can find them, have an instructor and an assistant at each station. Even if you have to use parents as assistants. I do this all the time and it works great for me.

Here is another technique that works great with young kids. They have a short attention span. So when you need to just talk to all of them, then make them sit down cross legged, Indian style, and in a semi circle around in front of you. They have less of a tendency to mess around, kick each other, and talk too much when you do it this way. Don't let them stand up, that's when the listening usually stops.

Stop, Side-Side, Forward-Back With the Feet (No.69)

This is just a simple little drill to get used to handling the ball with your feet. You will need 3 soccer balls and 3 positions. Rotate the players so that there is one player at each position. Say "GO", then the player at *position 1* straddles the ball with a foot on each side. Next they put the bottom of their right foot on the top of the ball. Then they quickly put it back down. Next they put the bottom of their left foot on the top of the ball, then back down. This counts as one turn. Have them do this 10 times in succession, then stop.

NOTE:

If you like, you can have them yell out the "turn number" each time as they complete it.

At the same time the player at *position 2* straddles the ball with both their feet about 6 inches away from the edge of the ball. On "GO"

they take the inside of their right foot and bump or push the ball over to the left foot. Then they take the left foot and push the ball all the way back to touching their right foot. This counts as one turn. Have them do this 10 times in succession, then stop.

At the same time the player at *position 3* straddles the ball with their feet on both sides. On "GO" they put the bottom toes of their right foot on the top of the ball. Next they roll the ball straight out in front with their toes about 12 inches away. Then very quickly they roll it back to the starting point. Next they repeat this with the toes of their left foot, out and back. This counts as one turn. Have them do this 10 times in succession, then stop.

Now the player at position 1 goes to position 2, and the next player in line goes to position 1. Position 2 goes to position 3. Position 3 player goes to the end of the line. Then you say "GO" and everything is repeated at each position. When they have done 10 reps, they rotate from position to position. This keeps going on for the whole 15 or 20 minutes. Everyone has to try each position Then the whole group rotates to the next station. So you end up with 3 ball handling moves being learned simultaneously. Run this drill at every practice with them until you observe the ball control has become automatic.

Hop Over, Jump Up, Roll Up Leg With the Feet (No.70)

This is another simple little drill to get used to handling the ball with your feet. Just a little more advanced. This is getting a lot of touches in a short period of time. You will need 3 soccer balls and 3 positions. Rotate the players so that there is always one player at each position.

Say "GO", then the player at **position 1** stands just to the right of the ball. Next they hop sideways over the ball, first to their left then back to their right. Alternate touching it lightly with the bottom of the foot each time as they go over. To the left and back to the right counts as one turn. Have them do this 10 times in succession, then stop.

At the same time the player at *position 2* straddles the ball with both their feet tightly against the edge of the ball. On "GO" they jump up high in the air, taking the ball with them between their feet. Then they come back down while keeping the ball between their ankles. This counts as one turn. Have them do this 20 times in succession, then stop.

At the same time the player at *position 3* straddles the ball with their feet on both sides. On "GO" they take the inside of their right foot against the ball and roll it 2 or 3 inches up the inside of their left leg, then back down. Next they do the same thing with their left leg, rolling the ball up the inside of their right leg. This counts as one turn. Have them do this 10 times in succession, then stop. All players should end about the same time. Have them go as fast as they can through the drill.

Now you rotate players, from position to position, then to the end of the line. This keeps going on for the whole 15 or 20 minutes. Everyone must try each position. Coaches instruct kids to work on the most important thing, their TECHNIQUE. Also at this point, after they have doing this a few practices, have them do it while NOT looking down at their feet. This develops control by feel. This teaches them to control the ball while looking and glancing around to see other things going on close to them.

Obstacle Dribbling (No.71)

This is another simple little drill to get them used to dribbling the ball around with their feet. This is getting a lot of touches in a short period of time. First set up a playing area using cones, either 20 x 30 yds. or 30 x 40 yds. depending on the number of kids.

Part 1 (*5-7 minutes*)

Each player has to dribble around inside of the area, using all the surfaces of their foot (make sure they do). They have to maintain control of the ball and stay inside of the area. They can not bump into other players. They have to stop with their foot on top of the ball when the coach yells FREEZE. They try to be in an open space away from other

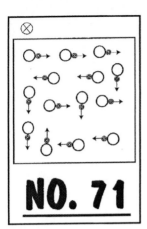

NO. 71

players when they hear freeze. They should move in a gentle jog, no walking and gentle touches on the ball.

Part 2 *(5-7 minutes)*

Divide onto two groups, then each group takes turns spread out and standing like statues. The other group (half) try to dribble around them.

Part 3 *(5-7 minutes)*

Divide onto two groups again, then each group takes turns spread out and standing like statues, but this time with their feet spread apart. The other group (half) dribbles up to them and passes the ball through their feet as they move around the area.

Stuck in the Mud Dribbling Game (No.72)

Part 1 *(7-10 minutes)*

Use the same size playing area as in No.71. Designate two players as "Monsters". Each player dribbles around the area using all surfaces of

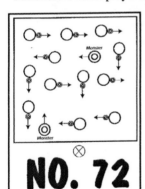

NO. 72

their feet (make sure they do). The two monsters attempt to tag the players. When tagged they are "stuck in the mud" and must hold the ball above their head and stand still with their feet apart. Any of the other players may free the tagged players by passing the ball through their feet. Make sure all players take a turn at being "monsters".

Part 2 *(7-10 minutes)*

Use the same size playing area as in No.72. Designate two players as "Monsters". Same as part 1 game except to free the tagged player, the other players have to pass the tagged player the ball, and they have to pass it back successfully to get free again.

Speed Dribbling Game (No.73)

Part 1 *(4 minutes or at least 2 x through per player)*

Use the same size playing area as in No.71. Divide into four equal teams. Players speed race against each other to dribble to the opposite end line, then go to the end of the line. When they all get to the other end, they wait for the last player, then they all race back the other way to the end where they started.

Part 2 *(4 minutes or at least 2 x through per player)*
Same as part 1 except players have to make a designated number of touches on the ball.

Part 3 *(4 minutes or at least 2 x through per player)*
Same as part 1 except players have to use their non-dominate foot (usually the left) once through. Coming back they alternate their dribble using both feet.

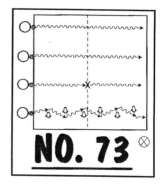

Part 4 *(4 minutes or at least 2 x through per player)*
Same as part 1 except players have to stop for at least several seconds on the half way line then continue on.

Part 5 *(4 minutes or at least 2 x through per player)*
Same as part 1 except players have to dribble race down to the other end, turn and dribble race back to starting line.

Part 6 *(4 minutes or at least 2 x through per player)*
Same as part 1 except add staggered cones to each lane for slalom dribbling all the way down and then all the way back.

Beat the Crabs Game (No.74)
Part 1 *(7-10 minutes)*
Use the same size playing area as in No.71. All the players line up at one end with a ball. Then they all attempt to dribble past the coach, who is in the "crab" position, all the way down to the other end.
When they all get there they come back the other way. The "crab has to stay in the middle, but they can roam side to side.

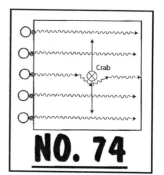

If the "crab" can trap the ball between their feet as the player tries to dribble past, then that player is out and also becomes a "crab". The players all have to weave in and out using the inside and outside of their feet as they dribble down to the other end. Eventually many become "crabs" and trap all the players. The last player left is the winner.

Part 2 *(7-10 minutes)*
Same as part 1 except the area is narrowed, maybe down to 15 yards wide. This is so that as they dribble it forces better control and closer dribbling.

King of the Hill Game (No.75)

This is a dribbling control and protect game. Put all your player's

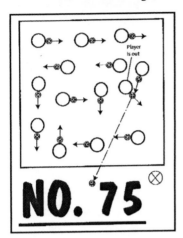

in a big area about 20 yds. wide x 30 yds. long marked with cones. Everyone has a ball. What each player has to do is continually dribble around the area with their ball while trying to knock the other player's ball out of the area.

When a player's ball is knocked out of the area, they are out of the game. The rule is each player has to attempt to attack another player's ball while defending their own. What you have to do is disqualify and send out any player that does NOT try to attack. The last player left is the winner.

Relay Passing Drill (No.76)

This is a basic passing drill to get used to passing a ball in different ways. Put all your players in a big area about 20 yds. wide x 30 yds. long marked with cones. You can make the area larger or smaller depending on the age of your kids if necessary. Divide players up into four rows. Put four players in the middle, and four players at the other end. Blow a whistle or say "GO." Each player in the front of the rows has a ball.

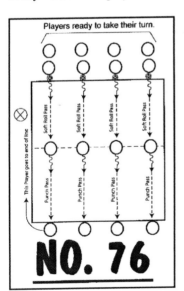

They start by dribbling the ball out 2 or 3 feet, then they make a "soft roll pass" to the player in the middle, using the inside of their dominate foot. The second time through they make this pass with outside edge of their dominate foot. The third time through they do the same thing, but with their non-dominate foot.

The middle player receives and controls the pass, turns, dribbles for 2 or 3 feet, then makes a firm "punch pass", toes bent, to the player at the end line. Each player follows their pass and takes the place of the player they just passed to, then gets ready to receive a pass.

The player at the end of the field picks up the ball, runs it back to the coach, and goes to the end of the line they started at. As soon as the starting player begins, the next player in line gets a ball and moves up ready to go again. In other words all the rows keep rotating. As soon as the ball almost gets to the third player at the end of the field, the next group can start. Keep the drill continually moving as long as all the players are set, this way more kids get more touches on the ball.

Partner Passing Drill (No.77)

This is a basic passing drill to get used to passing the ball to a specific player. Put all your players in a big area about 25 yds. wide x 35 yds. long marked with cones. You can make the area larger or smaller depending on the age of your kids if necessary. Divide players up into two groups of 6 or 7 players.

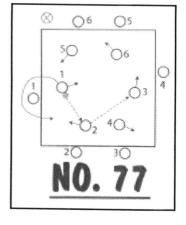

Put all the players on one group inside of the area. The other group is divided up around the outside edges of the area. Now, number all your players inside of the area from 1-7. Player No.1 has the ball.

Part 1 *(5-7 minutes)*
Blow a whistle or say "GO." Player 1 passes the ball to No.2, No.2 passes to No.3 and so on. The ball is continually passed to the next consecutive number player over and over. After passing, each player has to keep moving around inside the area. After each inside player has had a chance to make several passes, then rotate in all the outside players to inside the area.

Part 2 *(5-7 minutes)*
Blow a whistle or say "GO." Run this drill the same as part 1, except after each player has passed the ball to the next consecutive player they run outside around the nearest player then back inside, and keep moving around. Rotate players the same as in part 1.

Part 3 *(5-7 minutes)*
Make sure all outside players have a number. Inside and outside players with the same number partner up together. Blow a whistle or say "GO." Then run this drill the same as part 2, except after each player has passed the ball to the next consecutive player they run outside to the partner with the same number, and they switch. The partner then runs inside and becomes the inside player with the same number. And the drill goes on.

Pass Against a Defender Drill (No.78)

This is another basic passing drill to get used to passing the ball to a specific player while avoiding a defender intercepting the ball. Put all your players in a big area about 25 yds. square marked with cones. You

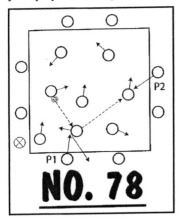

can make the area larger or smaller depending on the age of your kids if necessary. Divide players up into two groups of 6 to 8 players.

One group spreads out around the outside of the area, the other group spreads out inside the area.

Part 1 (5-7 minutes)

Blow a whistle or say "GO." One player inside then takes the ball and starts passing it around from team mate to team mate, and they all have to keep moving. Before starting, demonstrate to make sure all the inside players understand how to make the correct passing angles. Next at random, one player at a time from the outside sprints in and attempts to touch the ball.

They have 15 seconds inside the area to try and touch the ball as it is passed around, then they have run back out. Only one player at a time can run into the area. So it's in, attempt a touch, then out quickly. Any one of the outside players can run in, but NOT two at a time. The coach will have to keep track of the 15 second interval, who is in, who is out, and the score. Or get a parent to help you keep track of the scoring. The outside team scores 1 point each time they touch the ball. Or if the inside team can make 5 successful passes, they score 1 point.

Part 2 (5-7 minutes)

Blow a whistle or say "GO." Run this drill the same as part 1, except now make it harder to make a clean pass by letting two defenders in at a time to try for a touch.

Part 3 (5-7 minutes)

Blow a whistle or say "GO." Run this drill the same as part 1, except now make it harder to make a clean pass by limiting the players to make only a two touch pass.

Basic Hop and Plant Passing Drill (No.79)

This is another basic passing drill to get used to the "hop and plant" technique of passing. Put all your players in a big area about 25 yds. wide x 7 yards long marked with cones. You can make the area larger or smaller depending on the age of your kids if necessary. Divide players up into two groups of player's. One group goes over to the other side of the short length. Make 5 rows of players on each end. Each player on one end has a ball. Explain and show them how to make the hop and plant pass. Have them approach the ball and plant the non-kicking foot up next to the ball so that their toes are even with or past the back of the ball, and pointing at the target. Tell them DO NOT put the plant foot behind the ball. A small hop just before the foot is planted will give them a rhythm.

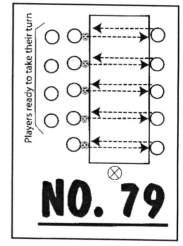

The object is a rolling type pass to the player opposite of them. That player receives and stops the ball. Next they go a few steps behind the ball, and make a "hop plant" pass back to their partner. The more coaches or parents you can have instructing, the quicker they will learn. Make sure all the little kids take their time and do it right.

The Name and Pass Drill (No.80)

This is another basic passing drill to get used to passing the ball quickly to a specific player. This is also a good drill for teaching communication skills. All your players get in a big circle and pass the ball to each other. Give one player the ball. That player yells out the name of a team mate then passes the ball to that player.

Before the ball gets there the receiving player must call out the name of someone in the circle and then, touching the ball only once, pass it to that player. If the real little kids and beginners are having trouble, then have them settle the pass first and make it a 2 touch pass.

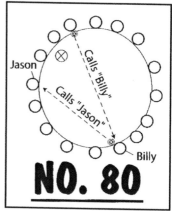

This teaches players to look up the field and then quickly pick out a receiver before they get to a loose ball. The smaller the circle is, it will then be easier for the little kids to make their pass.

The Short Looping Pass Drill (No.81)

This is another basic passing drill to get used to passing the ball quickly just a short distance to a specific player, but over the top of the head of an approaching opponent in front of them. Put all your players in a big area about 25 yds. wide x 7 yards long marked with cones.

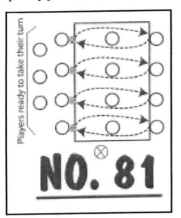

You can make the area larger or smaller depending on the age of your kids if necessary. Divide players up into three groups of players. One group goes down to the other end of the short length. The third group goes in the middle and just stands there. Make sure you rotate this middle group every few minutes so they get their turn.

Make 4 rows of three players across the area. Each player on one end has a ball. Explain and show them how to make the short looping pass. Sometimes referred to as a *"chip shot."* Have them approach the ball at an angle, and plants the non-kicking foot farther away from the side of the ball than they normally would. Then they lean backwards so that they can fully extend their kicking leg, and lift the ball. They strike the ball low, in a chopping motion, but they DO NOT follow through. As they start their kick have them keep their head down.

The object is a short looping type pass over the head of the middle player, and to the player on the end opposite of them. That player receives and stops the ball. Next they go a few steps behind the ball, and make a "looping" pass back to their partner. The more coaches or parents you can have instructing, the quicker they will learn. Make sure all the little kids take their time and do it right. Running this drill a lot, even for 15 to 20 minutes at a time, will help them make this a "muscle memory" learning experience. This technique also works for free kicks depending on the distance.

Duo or Trio Juggling Drill (No.82)

This is another basic drill just to get them used to juggling the ball off the surfaces of their body. Put all your players in Pairs facing each other, or in trio's in a big area about 25 yds. wide x 25 yards long.

Part 1 *(12-15 minutes)*

Have all the players pair up facing each other in rows about 6 -8 feet apart. First tell them which part of their body they can use to start out. Blow a whistle or say "GO." The coach yells, "Head," one player takes the ball,

78

throws it up, and one touch heads the ball up in the air over to their partner. The partner one touches heads the ball back. This is one turn. The player then one touch heads the ball back over the partner again. The partner one touch heads it back over, This is two turns.

After two turns the coach yells, "Thigh," the player now one touch juggles the ball over to the partner using their right thigh. The partner one touch juggles it back with their right thigh. Now the next time the player uses their left thigh to juggle it over. The partner left thigh juggles it back. This is two turns.

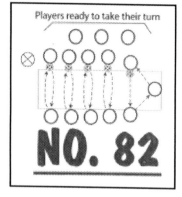

Now the coach yells, "Feet," and the player one touch juggles it over using the inside of their right foot. The partner one touch juggles it back with the inside of their right foot. The player then one touch juggles the ball over using the inside of their left foot. The partner one touch juggles it back with the inside of their left foot. Now the player's rotate and new player's move in and repeat the 3 parts of the body drill so that everyone gets a turn. Once your players get experience with this drill, run it faster, but if you need a little more time, take it. The real little kids may need 2 touches. That's OK until they get better.

Part 2 *(15-18 minutes)*

Have all the players get into triangles of three, in groups about 6 -8 feet apart. First tell them which part of their body they can use to start out. Blow a whistle or say "GO." Run this the same as part 1, except the ball goes around from player to player in the triangle. The coach yells, "Head," "Thigh," or "Foot." the same way. Each player gets two touches at each part of the body. It will probably help if the first player yells, "One," when the ball has been around to all three players one time. Don't forget to rotate if there are extra players so that they all get a turn.

Juggling for Height Drill *(No.83)*

This is a little more complicated drill. You may have to use this drill with the older kids. You can try this with the real litle kids, but I think it will be too hard for most of them. Again the object for juggling is keep the ball in the air as long as possible. To warm up they can use any part of their body, the feet, head, shoulders, chest or thighs, except NO HANDS. Let them warm up for about 5 minutes using as many parts of the body as possible.

After they get warmed up have each player juggle the ball and keep it below their knee using only their feet. Have them do this for about 2 or 3 minutes then change the rules. Next each player has to juggle the ball and keep it a little higher, but below their waist using only their feet. Do this for about 2 or 3 minutes. Next have each player juggle the ball higher, but keep it below their head using only their feet. Do this for about 2 or 3 minutes. And last have each player juggle the ball above their head using only their feet. Do this for about 2 or 3 minutes.

The next time you run the drill have each player keep the ball below their head, but this time using only their thighs. Then over their head with only using their thighs. What this does is build touch and concentration. Make sure they understand that the object is to keep every touch over or under the specified area. To make this drill more difficult, put all the players in a large square area marked by cones. This puts pressure on them to stay inside the area and avoid running into their fellow team mates.

Around the World Drill (No.84)

This is also a little more complicated drill. You may have to use this drill with the older kids. You can try this with the real litle kids, but I think it will be too hard for most of them. Again the object for juggling is keep the ball in the air as long as possible without touching the ground. To warm up they can use any part of their body, the feet, head, shoulders, chest or thighs, except NO HANDS or ARMS. Let them warm up for about 2 or 3 minutes using as many parts of the body as possible.

Now start the drill with each player getting a ball and a partner, then facing each other at about 6 feet apart. One player starts by juggling the ball with their right foot. Then they juggle the ball up to the right thigh. Then up to the right shoulder, and from there to their head. Then from the head down to the left shoulder, to the left thigh, to the left foot and then they juggle it over to their partner. The partner then goes through the same "around the world" routine. See which pair can continue the drill the longest 30 minutes without a drop. Now here is another thought. For fun and learning have several players from an older team come over and put on a demonstration for your young team. It will be fun, and they will be impressed.

The Rainbow Juggling Drill (No.85)

This is also a little more complicated drill. It's a form of juggling where the player flips the ball from behind them, and over their heads to in front of them. You may have to use this drill with the older kids or save it for later on when they get older. You can try this with the real litle kids, but

80

I think it will be too hard for most of them. Again the object for juggling is keep the ball in the air as long as possible without touching the ground. To warm up they can use any part of their body, the feet, head, shoulders, chest or thighs, except NO HANDS or ARMS. Let them warm up for about 2 or 3 minutes using as many parts of the body as possible.

Now start the drill with each player getting a ball and a partner, then facing each other at about 6 feet apart. Here is how it works. The player places the ball behind the heel of their left foot. The right foot reaches behind the ball, toes down, makes contact with the laces, and lifts the ball so that it rolls up the heel of the left foot.

The player then leans forward and catches the ball with the back of the left heel and ankle. Next they push off with the left foot and lift the ball quickly, kicking it over their head to their partner using the back of the left heel.

Now the partner faces them, goes through the same routine, and kicks the ball over their head back to their original partner. See which pair can continue to make the kick the longest and most times without a problem during this 30 minutes drill.

Wall Kicking Trap Drill (No.86)

This is a simple little basic drill for learning to trap the ball from a pass. You can send your players home to work on this drill or you can work on it as a two person team at practice. All they need to do this at home is a concrete wall or a large piece of plywood leaned against the wall at an angle. When the plywood is tilted back a bit, it rebounds the ball in the air. Have them trap some balls on the ground and some in the air. Basically they kick the ball hard against the wall or plywood sheet. When it bounces back they trap it. Tell them to remember to use the instep, the inside and outside of each foot, NOT just the dominate leg of foot. If it's a high bouncing ball tell them to use their shins on their legs to trap the ball.

At practice have your players line up in pairs facing each other. One player kicks or passes the ball to their partner. The partner traps it using all the parts of their feet. Then they kick or pass the ball back to their partner for them to trap. You can make a game out of this by scoring points for missed traps. The pair with the fewest points wins.

Trap-N-Pass Drill (No.87)

This is a simple little basic drill for learning to trap the ball from a pass or kick then relay it to a team mate, who traps it and moves it on. By

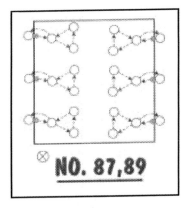

NO. 87,89

working in groups of three it will help your players offensive techniques. Put all your players in a big area about 35 yds. wide x 35 yards long marked with cones. You can make the area larger or smaller if necessary, depending on the age and number of your kids. Divide players up into groups of three . Spread them out in the area at about 5 yards apart from each other.

Explain and show them how to face the player overhead throwing the ball in to them, trap the ball, turn, and pass the ball to the next team mate. That team mate does the same thing, traps the ball, turns and passes it to the third player. The third player also traps, then turns and passes the ball back to the original player, who then kicks or passes the ball back to the player throwing it in.

To make the drill harder, after one or two times through, the coach can yell in how each player has to make the trap, inside of foot, outside of foot, instep or on the shin. Then each player has to trap it that way. Make them use their dominate foot and leg the first time, and the second time they have to use their weak leg and foot. If there are extra players waiting for their turn, then randomly substitute them in at different positions.

Tight Trap-N-Blast Drill (No.88)

This is a little drill for learning to trap the ball from up in the air, then sprint out dribbling with the ball at their feet for a short distance while weaving between players. Put all your players in a big area about 6 yds. wide x 10 yds. long marked with cones. You can make the area larger or smaller if necessary, depending on the age and number of your kids. If you don't have enough kids for the middle use cones for weaving through. Divide players up into groups of five. Put one on each end, spread the other three out in the middle.

Explain and show them how to throw the ball up, trap it when it comes down, then sprint dribble weaving between the three players in the middle. After they have weaved through the three players in the middle, they pass the ball off to the player waiting on the other end. That player catches the ball, then throws it up and does the same thing as the other player. The first time through they use their dominate leg and foot. The second time through they have to use their weak leg and foot.

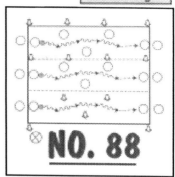

After each player gets two chances, rotate your players so that they all get at least two turns. If you have lots of players you may want to add more 2 yd. wide lanes, to get more players working in the shorter period of time that you have to practice in.

Receive-N-Pass Drill (No.89)

This is a simple little basic drill for learning to receive the ball from a pass or kick then relay it to a team mate, who receives it and moves it on. I'm working the receiving right in with the trapping because they are very similar. The big difference is that receiving is basically from the thighs up where trapping is usually considered from the shins down. By working in groups of three it will help your players offensive techniques. Put all your players in a big area about 35 yds. wide x 35 yards long marked with cones. You can make the area larger or smaller if necessary, depending on the age and number of your kids. Divide players up into groups of three in the middle. Spread them out in the area at about 5 yards apart from each other.

As in Drill No.87, explain and go over the types of more flat body areas they will be using to do the receiving, the thighs, chest and forehead. Tell your players that they have to control the ball in such a way that they lay it down right in front of them. Make sure they understand that they deaden the ball, and kind of catch it with their body so that it does NOT bounce 20 feet away at contact.

Run this drill almost exactly like No.87, except the players are receiving the ball with their thighs, chest or forehead. Start them out receiving with their thigh, then after several times through change it to the chest, then the forehead. They can start out with their dominate thigh, then make sure the next time they use their weak leg thigh. Don't forget to randomly rotate in any of the extra players so that they get a turn.

Receiving and Moving Drill (No.90)

This is a little drill for learning to receive the ball from a pass or kick then relay it to a team mate, who receives it and moves it on. I'm working the receiving right in with the trapping because they are very similar. The big difference is that receiving is basically from the thighs up

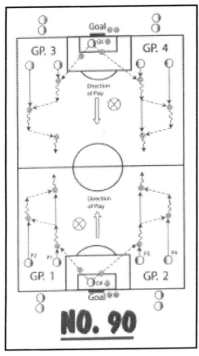

NO. 90

where trapping is usually considered from the shins down. If you have enough kids this is a full field drill. If not mark out an area about 30 yds. wide x 50 yds. long with cones, and run one group.

The goalkeeper or coach yells, "GO," and throws out a ball just a little in front of P1 who sprints out straight ahead. At the same time P2 sprints out straight ahead, running parallel to P1.

P1 receives the ball, brings it down, dribbles out a few yards and passes the ball over just a little ahead of P2. P2 receives the ball, brings it down, dribbles out a few yards then passes it back to the sprinting P1. P1 receives the ball back, brings it down, and dribbles out to the mid line.

They then pick up the ball, run it back around the side line back to the goalkeeper or coach. As soon as the first two players are almost down to the mid line a new group of two starts with the ball being thrown out. You can run 4 groups at once if you have a full field to work on. The idea is practicing passing and receiving while at a full all out sprint run.

Shoot at a Middle Goalkeeper Drill (No.91)

This is a little drill for learning to kick the ball past a goalkeeper and through the goal cones. The beauty of this drill is you can put your goalkeeper's in he middle between the cones and they can get some work. Here is how it works. All the players on one end get a ball, dribble out a few yards, then attempt to beat the goalkeeper to one side or the other with a kick. After kicking they retrieve the ball if they miss, then go around the goalkeeper to the end of the waiting line on the other side.

If the kick goes through between the cones, and the goalkeeper is ready, the next player comes up, dribbles out and tries for a goal. If the goalkeeper makes the stop and catches the ball, they hand it to the player going by, or they pass the ball to a player on the other end. When all the players get to the other side, the shooting starts again from that side.

The first time kicking have each player use their dominate foot. The next time kicking they have to use their weak foot. Then alternate every other time. This is how they will become versatile, handling the ball with either foot, and being able to shoot with either foot.

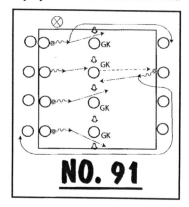

If you want to make the drill harder, have then dribble, spin turn and then shoot. Players should try to use the inside of their foot some of the time, and the instep (top on laces) some of the time.

Shooting Gallery Drill (No.92)

This is a little drill for learning to kick the ball past a goalkeeper and into certain parts of the goal. The beauty of this drill is you can put your goalkeepers in goal and they get some work also, instead of you in the goal. This is a must drill for your strikers and forwards. If you only have your shooters working on this, I would run this drill longer than normal. You probably want to have players work the hardest on ground ball shots. They are actually the hardest for the little kids to catch or stop. The best targets are the upper corners of the goal. For ground balls though the lower corners are the best. For familiarity and the best practice, use a full size goal for this.

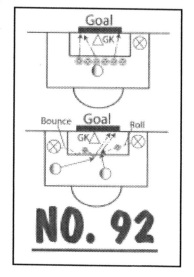

There are several approaches. One, you can line up a bunch of balls at different distances out in front of the goal, then aim your ground ball shots at different low targets. Two, you or a coach can throw rolling centering passes out in front of the goal. Three, you can throw a bouncing ball out in front of the goal so that they can try some one touch volley shots.

For the ground ball shots, show them how to hit the ball with the inside middle part of their foot, and dead center of the ball. They need to learn to keep their head down, and eyes on the ball. To get the ball up though you want to show them how to kick using their instep. First they need to curl their toes, but don't strike the ball to low or it will sail over the cross bar. It's matter of experience and feel to get the ball to go where you want it to go. For one touch volleys show them how to strike the ball at dead center on the side. This take lots of focus, and patience to learn. Work them long and hard because the more they shoot the better they get.

Shooting Stars Game (No.93)

This is a little game for fun and to encourage them to shoot goals.

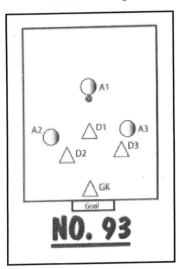

Set up an area about 15 yds. wide x 20 yds. long with a goal. A 6 yd. wide goal for the real little kids, an 8 yds wide goal for the older kids. Play 3 vs 3 with a goalkeeper. Playing 3 vs 3 each player should get a lot of touches. Award 1 point for each attempted shot, and 2 points for each goal.

Have each team play 15 minutes then switch sides so that each team gets a chance to score goals. The team with the most points after 30 minutes wins the game. You will need to referee to make sure the rules are followed. Basically just let them go at it though with free play, just no flagrant fouls allowed.

Give and Go Shooting Drill (No.94)

This is a little drill for learning how to shoot goals off "give and go" passes and bouncing drops for volley kicks. Set up an area about 15 yds. wide x 30 yds. long using

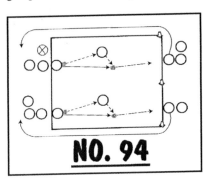

cones for two goal targets. You will need a passer in the middle, and a players on the other end in goal just to get the ball. Basically you have two groups so that you can get more kids working in a short period of time.

Make sure after all the players kicking in the first two groups get their chance that you rotate players in the middle so that they get a turn, then keep rotating so that everyone get multiple shots. The second time through at shooting have all players use their weak foot.

On the third time through the passer bounces a pass, and all players try for a volley shot on goal. This is where they make their shot when the ball bounces up just slightly in the air.

Back Pass Attack Shooting Drill (No.95)

This is a little drill to work on their passing to set up the shot. Set up an area about 30 yds. wide x 40 yds. long with a goal at each end using cones. A 6 yd. wide goal for the real little kids, an 8 yds wide goal for the older kids. Each end has a group of players and a goalkeeper. To get more kids working at the same time, you could set this whole group up two or three times across a big field.

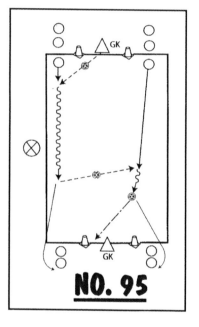

To get this drill going the goalkeeper on one end rolls the ball a little out in front of a player (attacker) in one of the lines. That attacker sprints out, catches up to the ball, receives it, then starts dribbling down the field. At the same time a player (attacker) across from them on the same end starts sprinting out, and runs parallel and just a little back from them as they go down the field..

About two thirds of the way down the field the attacker with the ball passes the ball backwards to the other attacker. That attacker receives the ball, dribbles in just a little closer, puts a fake on the goalkeeper, then shoots to the goal corner farthest away from the goalkeeper. Both players then go around the outside of the field to the back of the waiting lines on that end. Next the opposite end goalkeeper repeats the same drill. Alternate attacks from each end. Every other time have the shooter use their weak foot on their shot.

After running this drill several times change it a little bit. The first attacker plays "give and go" with the second attacker. Then about two thirds of the way down they make a crossing run, receive and shoot.

Basic Heading Drill (No.96)

This is a very basic little drill for your beginning players so they can work on learning their heading moves. Set up an area about 15 yds. square using cones. Divide players up into groups of two or by themselves. Spread them out all over the area. For beginning kids only let them use a lightweight ball of some type. Here are some choices:

- Balloons.
- Double end punching bag bladders.
- 7 to 8 Inch diameter coated foam balls.
- 7 to 8 Inch diameter soft beach balls.

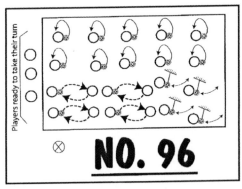

Part 1 *(5 minutes or at least 10 x per player)*
Make 4 rows of players across the area. Have them all kneel down so that they learn to NOT lunge or jump at the ball. They can start off each player having one or more balloons ready.

Explain and show them how to throw the ball straight up then make the header using only their forehead. With balloons they can see who can keep the ball in the air the longest.

With the other lightweight balls they can try to keep heading it straight up in the air, but it's going to be a little harder. Have then extend both arms about head height out to their front and sides. They can make a fist if they like, but tell them to make sure they only use their arms and hands as a balance guide for their forehead, but don't touch the ball with them.

Part 2 *(5 minutes or at least 5 x per player)*
Make 4 rows of players in pairs across the area at about 6 feet apart. Have them all kneel down. One player has a lightweight ball. Explain and show them how to throw the ball straight up with both hands, then make the header over to their partner using only their forehead. The partner catches the ball, throws it up, and heads it back to their partner. Emphasize keeping their neck bulled, their chin down, and arms extended for a balance guide.

Part 3 *(5 minutes or at least 2 x per player)*
To do this drill you will need to have a rope attached to the ball. I like to use a net around the ball to hold it. Allow enough room for the ball to swing. Tie the rope for 4 balls spread across the top goal cross bar, or find

88

some tree branches. Make 4 rows of players, one in front of each ball. They can stand for this part of the drill. Say "GO" and the players in front of a ball start to head the ball straight out in front of them, but NOT too hard.

It's going to swing and come back, so they have to be ready. When it comes back head it straight out in front again. They keep doing this for two hits then go to the end of the line as the players rotate. Emphasize using the same forehead techniques as in the other two drills.

A More Advanced Basic Heading Drill (No.97)

This is a very basic drill for your 12 year old players and up to work on to improve their heading moves and shooting. Set up an area about 15 yds. square using cones. Divide players up into groups of two or three players. Spread them out all over the area

When you use the middle player make sure you rotate them every few minutes so they get their turn at heading. For the best results keep these drills moving fast over and over. For all players use a No.4 soccer ball with some of the air let out. Or use a volleyball which is much lighter. It's a lot easier on their head and neck.

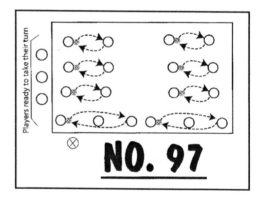

Part 1 *(3 minutes or at least 4 x through per player)*
Make 4 rows of two pairs of players across the area. Have them all kneel down so that they learn to NOT lunge or jump at the ball. One player in the pair has a ball. Explain and show them how to make the short header. One player throws the ball up in the air to themselves, then heads it over to their partner. The partner catches the ball the repeats the same thing heading back to the other player again. They keep doing this back and forth.

Part 2 *(3 minutes or at least 4 x through per player)*
One player underhand lobs the ball to their partner who is kneeling down, who then heads it back over to them. They do this for 3 or 4 times then switch and the other player underhands it over. This goes back and forth.

Part 3 *(3 minutes or at least 4 x through per player)*
One player kneels down, throws the ball up in the air to themselves, then heads it over to their partner. The partner kneels down then heads it right

89

back to them. Then they both try to make multiple headers back and forth to each other without the ball falling.

Part 4 *(3 minutes or at least 4 x through per player)*

One player throws the ball up in the air to themselves, then tries to head it past and around their partner for an imaginary goal. They do this for 3 or 4 times then switch and the other player throws it up and tries to head a goal past them. They keep doing this back and forth.

Part 5 *(3 minutes or at least 4 x through per player)*

Add a middle player for a group of three. The middle player lob throws the ball up in the air to one of the end players, who then heads it over the middle players head to their partner. The middle player turns around and lobs it over to the other end player to head it over them going back. It goes back and forth. Make sure to rotate the middle players so that they get a turn.

Heading Into the Goal Drill (No.98)

This is a drill for your teen age and up players to work on so they can improve their heading moves and shooting into the goal. Set up an area about 40 yds. square using cones. Each of the areas four sides has a regulation size goal, crossbar and everything. At each goal you have a goalkeeper, an attacker for the header, a ball feeder player and a chase

player. Make sure to rotate players and switch positions after 5 attempts at a goal.

Start with the feeder players P1, P3, P5 and P7 lobbing a ball up in the air so that the header players A1, A2, A3 and A4 can run up and head into the goal. The chase players P2, P4, P6 and P8 shag after the balls and get them over to the feeder players. If the goalkeeper makes a save, they can just roll the ball over to the feeder player.

After the 5 attempts have been made the attackers rotate to the chase player, the chase player becomes the feeder and the feeder becomes the attacking header player. You can rotate the goalkeepers, or you can just leave them in goal to get as much practice as possible. For the little kids the ball will probably have to be served or lobbed over. With the bigger kids the ball can be kick lobed over (option).

Faking Before/After the Pass Drill (No.99)

This is a basic drill for your players to learn how to fake on passing the ball. Set up an area about 15 yds. wide x 30 yds. long using cones. You will have attackers, receivers and defenders. Have two groups of players across the area. Each group will have one feeder, one attacker, and two defenders. The object of this drill is to work on faking before they receive the pass and after they receive the pass.

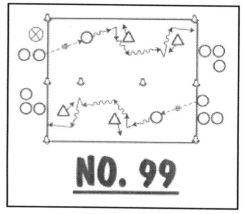

NO. 99

The feeder rolls the ball out to the attacker. The attacker either fakes or feints a move as they start running up the field, and before they receive the ball. Once they get the ball they either head fake, eye fake, or foot fake the first defender as they approach. What you want to teach them to do is pretend to go in one direction, get the defender to start to go in that direction, then the attacker goes the other way around.

For the real little kids have the defender actually move in the direction the player is pretending to go in. They can poke check at the ball, but they can NOT block the attacker from dribbling. The first defender does NOT chase after the attacker goes by. The attacker dribbles up towards the next defender does a feint, then head, eye, or foot fakes the second defender. Then they go around them and over the end line. The second defender does NOT chase either.

Next the drill plays out the same way, except it goes back the other way. Then both groups just keep going back and forth. Make sure you show them how to do the "slow and go" feint as well as the other head, eye and foot fakes. Just add more groups if you have too many players.

Faking Before/After the Goal Kick Drill (No.100)

This is a basic drill for your players to learn how to fake on getting into position, and faking on the actual kick. Set up an area about 15 yds. wide x 30 yds. long using cones. You will have attackers, defenders and goalkeepers. Have two groups of players across the area. Each group will have two feeders, two attackers, two defenders and a goalkeeper. The object of this drill is to work on faking before they receive the ball, and after they have the ball and they are ready to kick.

Both attackers A1 and A3 start out about midfield out on the wing. The attackers both start running towards the outside of the area. They both get their defenders D1 and D3 to commit to the outside, then they both cut back, and accelerate quickly towards the inside, and run around the defender. Just after they do, the feeders P1 and P3 roll feed the

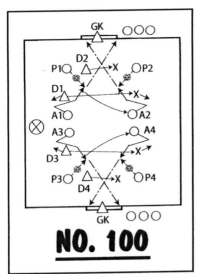

NO. 100

ball just out in front of them. Then they immediately put a head, eye, foot, or body fake on D2 and D4, then shoot low into the corner.

Next both players flip flop to the opposite side, become A2 and A4, then the drill repeats itself over there. After that two new attackers come up. Don't forget to rotate all the players inside the area and outside so that they all get an opportunity to work on it also. Make sure all your player know their fakes and feints.

For the real little kids have the defenders actually move in the direction the player is pretending to go in. They can poke check at the ball, but they can NOT block the attacker from running around them. The first defender does NOT chase after the attacker goes by. The second defender can mark but NOT block the shooter. After the kick is made, then make sure both defenders and the feeders immediately flip flop to the opposite side so that the drill keeps moving. Rotate all players often.

Down Field Faking Drill (No.101)

This is a basic drill for your players to learn how to fake on just passing the ball down the field. Set up an area about 15 yds. wide x 30 yds. long using cones. You will have attackers, receivers, passers and defenders. Have two groups of players across the area. Each group will have one feeder, two attackers, and two defenders. The object of this drill is to work on faking after they receive the pass.

The feeder rolls the ball out to the attacker. The attacker feints a move as they start dribbling up the field, then after they receive the ball they do either head fake, eye fake, or foot fake on the first defender as they approach, then pass back to the second attacker. What you want to teach them to do is pretend to go in one direction, get the defender to start to go in that direction, then the attacker goes the other way. The second attacker dribbles a short distance, waits for the first attacker to clear, then passes the ball back to them.

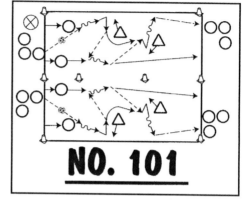

NO. 101

The attacker dribbles up towards the next defender does a feint, then head, eye, or foot fakes the second defender. They then go around them and kick the ball over the end line. For the real little kids have the defender actually move in the direction the player is pretending to go in. They can poke check at the ball, but they can NOT block the attacker from dribbling. The first defender does NOT chase after the attacker goes by. The second defender does NOT chase either.

Next the drill plays out the same way, except it flip flops and goes back the other way. Then both groups just keep going back and forth. You get more practice in this way. Make sure you show them how to do the "slow and go" feint as well as the other head, eye and foot fakes. Just add more groups if have too many players.

Basic Shielding Drill (No.102)

This is a basic drill for your players to learn how to shield the ball from a defender. Set up an area about 30 yds. square using cones. You will have attackers and defenders. Have all your players split up into pairs across the area. This is one on one shielding the ball from a defender.

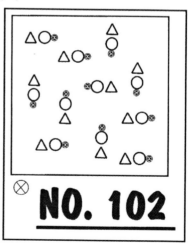

NO. 102

Part 1 (5 minutes)

The object of this drill is to control the ball with the outside foot while the defender provides constant passive pressure. Keeping themselves between the ball and the defender, they use both feet and change positions every 30 seconds.

Part 2 *(5 minutes)*

The object of this drill is the same as part 1, except now the defender is allowed to poke check at the ball with their toe.

Part 3 *(5 minutes)*

The object of this drill is the same as part 1, except now the defender is allowed to use full pressure to attempt to knock the ball away or steal it. Then after 1 minutes time you or one your coach yells, "Change," and all defenders immediately switch to another player to guard (mark).

Part 4 *(5 minutes)*

The object of this game is the same as part 1 drill, shield the ball and keep it away from the defender. You will need 8 attackers, each with a ball, to dribble around the area. You will need 4 defenders to try and take the ball away from them. If one of the players loses their ball, they are out of the game. The last player with a ball wins. It should be fun. The last player has to fight off 4 defenders.

Pass and Shield Drill (No.103)

This is a basic drill split up into several parts for your players to learn how to shield the ball from a defender after they get a pass. It also includes combining and passing off to another attacker who shields and passes off back and forth to the first attacker until either one can get over the end line with the ball. Set up an area about 15 yds. wide x 30 yds. long

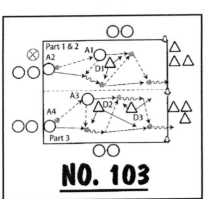

using cones. You will have attackers and defenders. Have all your players split up into two groups, and run each part on both sides across the area.

Part 1 *(7 minutes)*

This is one on one shielding the ball from a defender. The object of this drill is for A1 to control and shield the ball with the outside foot for 20 seconds while they quickly move around the area, and the defender D1 provides constant pressure. Keeping themselves between the ball and the defender, they have to use both feet. This is a high energy fast drill. Change and rotate in a new attacker and defender after every 60 seconds. Use your whistle to indicate every 60 second time interval.

Part 2 *(7 minutes)*

The object of this drill is the same as part 1, except a second attacker A2 comes in as support. They combine with each other to get the ball to the end line

94

Part 3 *(5 minutes)*

The object of this drill is the same as part 1 and 2, except now the defender D3 is added. Now the drill goes to 2 vs 2 play to the end line.

Get Away Moves Drill (No.104)

This is a basic drill to work on all the different foot, fake moves and feints to help your players get away from a defender. Set up an area about 15 yds. wide x 30 yds. long using cones. You will have attackers and defenders. Have all your players split up into three groups, and run each group over and over for a ONE HOUR time period, no more though. Then move on to another drill. Make sure to rotate all attackers and defenders for one rotation.

Each attacker gets a ball and moves all the way through to the end line dribbling and getting away from the defender. Go through one rotation of each move, then stop and go to the next move. There are many moves. Go through as many as you can at a session. You will have to keep track, then go to a different group of moves each week. This takes a lot of time, but it will be worth it. For the real little kids pick out 4 or 5 of the more simple moves to work on. Kids from 12 years old and up need to know how to perform all these moves using their feet. For how to perform each move go to the "reference" section.

Throw-Ins Drill (No.105)

This is a basic drill to work on the throw-in techniques for your players. One of the few times they get to use their hands. Set up an area about 15 yds. wide x 25 yds. long using cones. You will have a thrower, receivers and defenders.

Have all your players split up into two groups, and run each group over and over for the 40 minute time period so

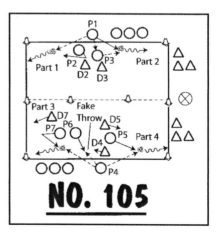

that all players get a chance to work on each of the four techniques. Then move on to another drill because little kids get bored. Make sure to continually rotate all thrower's, receivers and defenders for each part on both sides. The key is keep things moving at a fast pace.

Part 1 *(10 minutes)*

Have player P2 face the thrower P1 and either receive the throw-in direct or turns, fakes D2, then breaks up field to receive a long throw.

Part 2 *(10 minutes)*

P1 makes a throw right to the feet of P3, who taps the ball right back to P1 as they run in. P1 receives the pass in bounds, then dribbles up the field along the side line.

Part 3 *(10 minutes)*

P7 makes a break up field which pulls D7 with them. Then suddenly they turn, and cut back to receive a short pass from P4.

Part 4 *(10 minutes)*

D4 is standing right in front of P4. P6 breaks right towards the thrower P4, who fakes a throw by just looking right at them. This should draw D4 out of position. P4 then turns and makes the throw to P5 who has made a break towards the side line.

Wind Sprint Ladders Drill- Suicides (No.106)

All soccer players except maybe the goalkeeper need to do a lot of running. This is for endurance, speed and acceleration. This is a short coarse to get more running in during a short period of time. Use cones as markers to set up a 30 yard coarse.

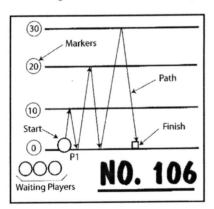

How this works is you blow your whistle, then each player runs 10 yds. and back, then 20 yards and back, then all the way out 30 yds. and back. Each time they get out even with the yard marker they have to reach down with one hand, touch the ground, pivot and run back to the starting point. They also touch down with one hand every time at the starting line.

One time through for everyone, and at least once a week if possible. If you really want to get fancy, then use old white one gallon milk cartons filled with sand or kitty litter. Mark the distance on each one with a wide tip black permanent marker pen (0, 10, 20, 30).

Running Laps Drill (No.107)

All soccer players except maybe the goalkeeper need to do a lot of running. This particular drill is for endurance. It's pretty simple. Start out your practice by running all your kids around the playing field for two laps. Not only are they building up their running endurance, but they are getting all their muscles warmed up. The better they get, the faster you can set the pace. Oh yes, always put your best runners out in front.

Running Backwards and Forwards Drill (No.108)

All soccer players except maybe the goalkeeper need to do a lot of running. This particular drill is great for back pedaling then turning and running forward without falling (coordinated running). This is a good change of pace running drill to use once in a while. And it helps them with their defensive marking. 10 or 15 minutes of this is all you need. Then move on.

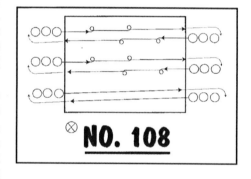

NO. 108

Put all your kids in three rows in a 30 x 40 Yd. area. First time down and back they all run backwards. Some will fall down, especially the real little kids. Do it with them and fall down yourself on purpose a few times so that they will all see it's not easy at first. Keep doing it, they will get better.

Next time down they run out about 10 yards backwards and then you blow a whistle. When they hear the whistle they turn around at a full run and go forwards. When they have ran another 10 yards or so, blow your whistle again. When they hear that they turn around again at a full run and run backwards again. They keep doing this about every 10 or 15 yards. The better they get the faster they have to run.

To speed up the drill, the player at the other end starts out when the runner passes them. They go to the end of the line when they finish their run. Then eventually they go back the other way. After a whole season of this they will all be very good at it. I have seen it happen.

The Direct Free Kick Drill (No.109)

All soccer players except maybe the goalkeeper need to learn how to make the direct free kick. Go back and look at No.20 play diagram. Line up your players this way, and have them take turns trying to make the kick from different angles around the penalty area the way I have shown.

97

Have your extra players form the wall. Have the kicker work the goal corners and do the fakes. Let each player take 2 different angle kicks at the goal, then rotate the players so that everyone gets a chance to make the kick or be one of the support players.

The Indirect One Touch Free Kick Drill (No.110)

All soccer players except maybe the goalkeeper need to learn how to make the one touch indirect free kick. Go back and look at No.21 play diagram. Line up your players this way, and have them take turns trying to make the kick from different set up angles around the penalty area the way I have it shown. Have your extra players form the wall. Have the kicker and your support players work the goal corners and do the fakes. Let each player take 2 different angle kicks at the goal, then rotate the players so that everyone gets a chance to make the kick or be one of the support players.

The Indirect Two Touch Free Kick Drill (No.111)

All soccer players except maybe the goalkeeper need to learn how to make the two touch indirect free kick. Go back and look at No.22, 23 and 24 play diagrams. Line up your players this way, and have them take turns trying to make the kick from different set up angles around the penalty area the way I have it shown. Have your extra players form the wall. Have the kicker and your support players work the goal corners and do the fakes. Let each player take 2 different angle kicks at the goal then rotate the players so that everyone gets a chance to make the kick or be one of the support players.

The Penalty Kick Drill (No.112)

All soccer players except maybe the goalkeeper need to learn how to make the penalty kick. Go back and look at No.25 play diagram. Line up your players this way, and have them take turns trying to make the kick from the penalty mark the way I have it shown. Have your five extra support players charge the goal as soon as the kick is made. Have the kicker and your support players work the goal corners, do the fakes and the deflection shots. Let each player take 2 kicks at the goal, then rotate the players so that everyone gets a chance to make the kick or be one of the support players.

The Corner Kick Drill (No.113)

All soccer players except maybe the goalkeeper need to learn how to make the corner kicks. Go back and look at No.15 thru No.19 play diagrams. Line up your players the different ways I have them shown, then have them take turns trying to make the kick from both corners the way I have them shown. Have your extra support players move around in the different positions I show. Have your support players work the goal corners on kicks, try the headers, do the fakes and the deflection shots. Let each player take 2 kicks at the goal, one from each corner, then rotate the players so that everyone gets a chance to make the kick or be a support player.

Defensive Skill Training Activities (Drills)

All drills will also be numbered for "EASY " reference.

The defensive drills will cover all the types of skills that young kids playing Soccer need to know to get started off on the right foot. Some are "Core Training" and most all involve "Muscle Memory" training. What you have to do is train the body and feet of your kids to make certain moves that will make them a better Soccer player. The skill activity drills are numbered so that you can have your assistant coaches use them and become more familiar with them for reference purposes between you, them and the kids.

These drills will cover the very basic fundaments like marking, blocking, tackling and goalkeping. We will also try to cover some special techniques that will help them. The plan with teaching these drills is stay with small group stations when possible where you or one of your coaches is teaching one of these skills. Keep the time period short, maybe 15 -20 minutes. Then blow a whistle and that group moves to the next station to learn another skill. The size of your groups will depend on how many kids you have on your team, and how many instructors you have. Many of the drills though you will have the whole team split up in groups on the field

As an example if you have 20 kids on your team, then you could have 4 groups of 5. And then you would need 4 stations and at least 4 instructors. The bigger your group is the more problems you will have. Smaller groups mean more touches. If you can find them, have an instructor and an assistant at each station. Even if you have to use parents as assistants. I do this all the time and it works great for me.

Here is another technique that works great with young kids. They have a short attention span. So when you need to just talk to all of them, then make them sit down cross legged, Indian style, and in a semi circle around in front of you. They have less of a tendency to mess around, kick each other, and talk too much when you do it this way. Don't let them stand up, that's when they are not listening as well.

Basic Marking Drill (No.114)

All soccer players except maybe the goalkeeper need to learn how to mark (cover) an offensive player with the ball. Explain to your players that marking usually takes place in the half of the where the goal they are defending is located. What they are doing is pressuring ball carriers, and staying close to them to deny passes to them within their defensive zone.

Tell them that they can't let a player stay unmarked anywhere in their own zone or near their goal. Set up an area 20 yds. wide x 20 yds. long marked by cones.

Part 1 (10 minutes)

Put 5 pair groups in the area, spread out. The five players dribbling try to get to the far side end line without losing the ball to the defender. The

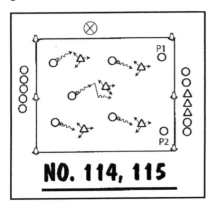

NO. 114, 115

defenders attempt to just stay between the ball and the end line. No stealing, blocking or tackling allowed in this particular drill. After 5 minutes, blow your whistle and rotate in 10 new players.

Part 2 (10 minutes)

This is the same as part 1 except the dribblers try to make a pass to either P1 or P2. The defenders mark, but also attempt to block or deflect any passes to P1 or P2.

Basic Blocking Drill (No.115)

All soccer players except maybe the goalkeeper need to learn how to "block tackle" offensive players with the ball from getting around them or being clear to make a pass. This is sometimes referred to as "ground" tackling. Explain to your players that marking usually takes place in the half of the where the goal they are defending is located.

I'm calling this "blocking", but it's really a form of tackling. What they are doing is pressuring ball carriers, staying close to them, then denying them passing opportunities to one of their team mates by blocking the ball. Tell them to use this technique when the player is dribbling directly at them. Teach them to stagger their feet, then use the inside of either foot up against the ball to block it. Have them alternate feet on each block.

Set up and run this drill just like No.114 part 1 and 2. The only difference is they will block tackle instead of just marking their opponent. Same time on the drill, and same rotation of the players.

Poke Tackling/Marking Monster Game (No.116)

All soccer players except maybe the goalkeeper need to learn how to "poke tackle" an offensive player with the ball. Explain to your players that poke tackling can take place just about anywhere on the field where the opportunity presents itself. What they are doing is pressuring ball carriers, staying close to them, denying them passing lanes in their zone, then looking for a mistake so that they can poke the ball away and make a steal. Have them alternate feet every time they attempt a tackle. This way they learn to use both feet.

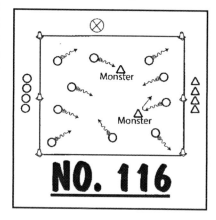

Remind them that they can't let a player stay unmarked anywhere in their zone or near their goal. Set up an area 20 yds. wide x 30 yds. long marked by cones. What I am going to do here is make a game out of this so that it will be more fun while they learn, especially the little kids.

Part 1 (10 minutes)

Put 10 players in the area, each with their own ball, and spread out. Put two players called "Monsters" in the area. Each player dribbles around the area and tries to stay away from the monsters. The monsters run around the area and try to stand right in front of a dribbling player. In this part though they can't touch the ball. This will help defenders getting used to chasing players and just getting in front of them. After 5 minutes, blow your whistle and rotate in all your extra players or 12 new players.

Part 2 (10 minutes)

This is the same as part 1 except the "Monsters" are now allowed to take the ball away from the dribblers. If the monster can take the ball away, then that player becomes a monster. Two or more monsters can not go after the same player (Double team them) though. After 5 minutes, blow your whistle and rotate in all your extra players or 12 new players.

Part 3 (Until Monsters eliminate all the dribblers)

This is the same as part 2 except the "Monsters" now poke tackle (kick) the ball away from the dribblers. If the monster can poke tackle the ball away, then that player is eliminated from the game, and immediately goes out of the area. Two or more monsters can not go after the same player (Double team them) though. Keep rotating in all your extra players as new dribblers when one of the dribblers is eliminated. Do this until all players get into the game.

101

Shoulder Tackle Drill (No.117)

All soccer players except maybe the goalkeeper need to learn how to make tackles on an offensive player with the ball. This is two players running side by side and both going for the ball. This is a technique

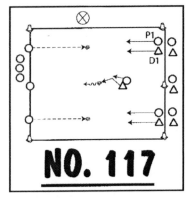

for the defender to get the ball. You will have an offensive player and a defensive player paired up. Set up an area 20 yds. square. Split up into 3 groups or rows. P1 and D1 on one end and a feeder player on the other end.

Blow your whistle or say "GO" and each feeder rolls the ball out to the center. At the same time each pair sprints out, and tries to gain possession of the ball and control it. The defender uses a shoulder tackle, being careful to keep their elbows in but using their body to keep the opponent from getting ahead to the ball. Make sure you rotate all players so that each on gets a chance to shoulder tackle. When all your players get to one end, then send feeders to the other end and run the drill the other way. You should run this drill only 20 to 30 minutes maximum.

Side Tackle Drill (No.118)

All soccer players except maybe the goalkeeper need to learn how to make tackles on an offensive player with the ball. Set this up in a 20 yrd. square area. This is two players running side by side, one dribbling the other attempting a tackle. This is a technique for the defender to get possession You will have an offensive player and a defensive player paired

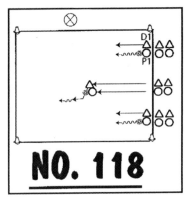

up. Split up into 3 groups or rows. P1 and D1 on one end.

Blow your whistle or say "GO." Each offensive player (P1) starts to dribble straight ahead. Each defender (D1) runs right beside of them. Somewhere about in the middle the dribbler attempts to kick the ball straight ahead.

The defender watches, then just as the kicker starts to kick they touch shoulders with elbows in. Next they step out and block the ball with

102

either the inside or outside of their foot. They do this with one part of the foot, and their body, in such a way that the ball remains in their possession. Make sure you rotate all players so that each one gets a chance to side tackle. When all your players get to one end, then they all turn around and do it the other way. You should run this drill only 20 to 30 minutes maximum.

Hook & Slide Tackle Drill (No.119)

All soccer players except maybe the goalkeeper need to learn how to make tackles on an offensive player with the ball. Set this up in a 20 yrd. square area. Hook tackling is used when the players are facing each other. Slide tackling is used when the dribbler has escaped the tackler, who remains right at their heels.

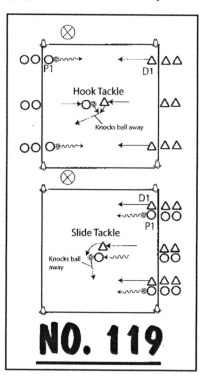

This is a technique for the defender to knock the ball away. The little beginning kids are going to have trouble with this technique, but you can try it with them. Set up an area 20 yds. wide, but only 15 yds. long. Split up into 3 groups or rows.

Part 1 *(10 minutes)*
You will have an offensive player and a defensive player paired together. They face each other on opposite ends of the area for the "hook tackle". Blow your whistle or say "GO". The offensive player (P1) starts to dribble straight ahead. The defender (D1) runs right at them.

Somewhere about in the middle the dribbler attempts to go around them. The defender confronts them at a slight angle and in a low position, then just waits to see which way they will go. When the opponent moves the ball to the side, the defender tries to move the ball out of the reach of the opponent with a drop down split hook like movement. Keep the drill moving fast. After one rotation, go back the other way from the opposite end.

Part 2 *(10 minutes)*
You will have an offensive player and a defensive player paired together. They start out side by side at one end line for the "slide tackle". Blow your

103

whistle or say "GO." P1 dribbles the ball straight ahead, with D1 right at their heels. It's important here that you tell your dribblers not to go too fast so that D1 can stay right at their heels. Somewhere about in the middle the tackler D1 puts on a burst of speed, starts down in a baseball like slide and attempts to contact the ball with the top foot, and the bottom foot is tucked under.

If it's a right footed dribbler, it may be advantageous to come on the left side of the dribbler. Just the opposite for left footed dribblers. Then just when the dribblers right foot starts to contact the ball is when they swing their top foot out and nudge or knock the ball away. It's very important here that you tell your defenders that they MUST contact the ball and not the opponents foot or leg, or it's a foul.

It's a judgement and timing thing. If they don't think they can make the tackle, then they should not try it. If they miss, then P1 keeps dribbling to the end line and goes to the end of the waiting line. D1 follows them to the end of the line also. Keep the drill moving fast. After one rotation, go back the other way from the far end. Keep the drill moving fast.

Goalkeeping Drill (No.120)

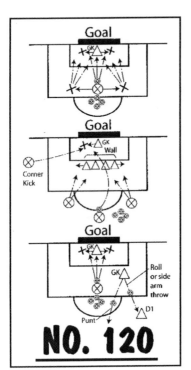

All goalkeepers need to learn the moves and techniques. You need to work them constantly. They will get to test these technique if you use them in other player drills, but this is where you or one of your coaches just works with goalkeepers.

As I mentioned previously, I would pick 3 or 4 players and train them as goalkeepers right from the beginning age groups. Set up a 6 yard wide goal for the little beginning kids for practice and an 8 yard wide goal (Std.) for the older kids. Each part of this drill is for a different move or technique.

Don't just push this drill off to anyone. It's extremely important that somebody works with your goalkeepers at every practice. You might also want to set up some hand signals so that they will know what you want them to do, just in certain special cases.

Part 1 *(10 minutes)*

You will have a goalkeeper and a coach, or possibly another goalie helping in case you don't have enough coaches The coach or helper needs lots of balls, to keep the drill moving fast. You get more work in that way. This part is working on catching and punching while on their feet. On low ground balls teach them to get in front of the ball then go down on one knee. They can also learn to use goalie gloves if it will help them.

Stand about in the middle of the penalty area, then on both sides and throw or kick balls right at the your goalkeeper. Throwing the ball will work better for the real little beginning kids. Then throw balls to each side of them. The first time they catch them using both hands. The second time they punch the ball to the sides. That's six balls to each goalkeeper, then rotate your goalkeepers.

Part 2 *(10 minutes)*

This is the same as part 1, except you throw the balls just a little out of their reach. They have to dive out and catch the ball using both hands. They dive for the ball on each side, then they dive and punch the ball away on each side. That's 4 balls to each goalkeeper, then rotate them.

Part 3 *(10 minutes)*

This is jumping and leaping for high balls that start to go over their head. Now here it gets tricky. They have to learn when to leap up and catch the ball, or when it appears to be a little to high to catch they tip the ball back behind them and over the cross bar using the palms of both hands. They will only learn this with lots of practice. That's 5 balls to each goalkeeper, then rotate them.

Part 4 *(10 minutes)*

This is teaching your goalkeeper to position a wall on free kicks. Lots of coaches don't use this, but it can be effective and kids should know how it works. Basically the wall is set up along the front edge of the goal area box. How many players are needed in the wall will depend on where the kick is coming from. If the kick is coming from the side, you may only need 3. If the kick is coming from the penalty arc, you may need 7 or 8.

Use your taller tough kids for the wall. They CAN'T use their hands and they just have to let the ball hit their body, it could be even in the face. What they have to do is keep their hands at their sides, and jump straight up to try and deflect the ball from getting past them. Your goalkeeper usually stands behind them in case the kick is looped over the wall. Teach your goalkeeper to position the center of the wall in front and in line with the kicker. They can say, "Wall left," or "Wall right." That's 5 balls kicked at the goal, then rotate all players to a different position..

Part 5 *(10 minutes)*

This is teaching your goalkeeper to distribute the ball. That is quickly getting rid of it when they make a save. When they get the ball have them quickly get away from the crowd of players and move out into a clear space somewhere in the penalty area. They look for a team mate not covered, and quickly roll or side arm throw the ball to them. If all their team mates are covered, then they kick or punt the ball into a clear space as far down the field as possible. That's 5 balls distributed out, then rotate all players to a different position.

Part 6 (10 minutes)

This is teaching your goalkeeper to work on stopping a penalty kick. You can use your extra goalkeepers or players to do the kicking. This is basically using the other techniques like catching, diving and tipping. The penalty kick comes from the penalty spot, the kicker is close so they come hard and fast. The goalkeeper has to learn to react quickly. Have them stay just in front of the goal, then face and line up with the kicker. That's 5 balls, then rotate all players to a different position.

Part 7 (10 minutes)

This is teaching your goalkeeper to work on stopping corner kicks. You can stand off to the side and simulate a corner kick coming in front of the goal. For the little kids I would throw the ball to different spots. Also throw them from both sides. For the older kids you could actually place several kids right in front of the goal, then have them head the ball towards the goal. This gives your goalkeeper a chance to see how to react to headers. That's 5 balls, then rotate all players to a different position.

Part 8 (10 minutes)

This is teaching your goalkeeper to work on stopping a direct and indirect free kicks outside of the penalty area. You can use your extra goalkeepers or players to do the kicking. This is basically using the other techniques like catching, diving and tipping. The goalkeeper has to learn to react quickly. Have them stay just in front of the goal, then face and line up with the kicker. That's 5 balls, then rotate all players to a different position.

Sweepers Drill (No.121)

I'm putting this here because more and more teams are using a sweeper these days, even some of the younger teams. I like to think of a "sweeper" as kind of a goalkeeper with limited rules. The biggest one is they can't us their hands. Think of them like they are a center fullback or stopper that stays way back. Their job is to stay way back near the goal and help the goalkeeper by backing up balls or players that break through, and intercepting any through balls then sweeping them away.

Some coaches say don't use a sweeper with a young beginning team because they stay back all the time and don't become comfortable around the ball in traffic. That could be the case with your team. It's your decision. As with goalkeepers, I would train maybe only 3 or 4 of your smarter faster players.

All sweepers need to learn the special moves and techniques they use. If you are going to use a sweeper, you need to work them constantly. The could save a tight game for you. Start out by setting up right in front of the goal because that is where they play. Take some cones and set up a shooting line just for reference in this drill.

Part 1 *(10 minutes)*

This is teaching your sweeper to work on intercepting a pass to a charging CF2. Blow a whistle or say "GO" and have CF1 start to dribble in towards the goal area. Have CF2 in place. At about the time CF1 is almost to them, have CF2 sprint towards the goal. D1 comes out to challenge CF1. CF1 the attempts to make a rolling pass to open space just in front of the line of cones.

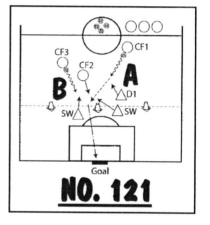

The sweeper anticipates the pass, runs over and intercepts the ball *(SEE FIGURE 121-A)*. If the sweeper misses the intercept, then CF2 kicks the ball into the goal.

Just for this drill the rule is CF2 can NOT get the ball way back of the line of cones and attempt a shot on goal. If they get the ball way back of the line they have to try and dribble in to the line of cones. Give the sweeper 5 chances at an intercept, then rotate all the players to a different position.

Part 2 *(10 minutes)*

This is teaching your sweeper to work on coming up and challenging a charging center forward, and attempt to block or tackle the ball. Have CF3 in place. Blow a whistle or say "GO" and have CF3 start to dribble in towards the goal area. At about the time CF3 is about 3 or 4 yards from the line of cones, have your sweeper go out right at them and try to get control of the ball. Just for this drill the rule is CF3 can NOT attempt to shoot the ball way back of the line of cones. They have to try and dribble in to the line of cones then shoot. Give the sweeper 5 chances at a block or tackle, then rotate all the players around.

Reference Section for Ball Control (Drills)

All the different moves will also be numbered for "EASY " reference.

This section is here to describe all the different moves soccer players can learn for controlling the ball. Some are "Core Training" and most involve "Muscle Memory" training. What you have to do is train the body and feet of your kids to make certain moves that will make them a better soccer player when dribbling a ball. The skill activity drills are numbered so that you can have your assistant coaches use them and become more familiar with them for reference purposes between you, them and your kids.

All moves assume you are a right footed dribbler. Left footed dribblers are flip flopped or opposite.

Inside Hook Turn Instructions (No.122)

1. Start by dribbling the ball forward about 4 yards.
2. Slow down and shorten your strides as you come up to your turning point.
3. Reach around the far side of the ball with the inside of your right foot. Inside of your left foot for left foot dribblers.
4. Using a sharp cut pivot with the inside of your right foot, turn your body 180 degrees around.
5. Pivot on your left foot so that you face back in the direction you came from.
6. Remember to come into the turn slow, then come out very fast.

Outside Hook Turn Instructions (No.123)

1. Start by dribbling the ball forward about 4 yards.
2. Slow down and shorten your strides as you come up to your turning point.
3. Plant your left foot, then reach around the far side of the ball with the outside of your right foot.
4. Next, pull the toes up on your right foot and turn it as far to the right as possible.
5. Using a sharp cut pivot with the outside of your right foot, flick the ball 180 degrees around so it goes in the opposite direction.
6. Now lean and turn your whole body back towards the ball.
7. Remember to come into the turn slow, then come out very fast.

Drag Back Turn Instructions (No.124)

1. Start by dribbling the ball forward about 4 yards.
2. Slow down and shorten your strides as you come up to your turning point.
3. Plant your left foot next to the ball, then place your right foot right on top of the ball.

4. Next, using the sole of your right foot move the ball with enough

5. As you do, make sure you open up your shoulders to let the ball roll across in front of your feet.

6. Now turn around facing the rear while your eyes are on the ball at all times.

7. Next catch up quickly to the ball, push it away from your feet and accelerate away.

The Puskas Move Instructions (No.125)

1. Start by standing right behind the ball.

2. Then using your right foot, place it on top of the ball and drag it backwards alongside your standing foot.

3. As you do this hop backwards so that your standing foot is always well behind the ball.

4. To complete the move, use your right foot to push the ball away at an angle you want to go in.

5. Now explode out at that angle for about 4 yards to finish.

The Spin Turn Instructions (No.126)

1. Start by dribbling the ball forward about 4 yards.

2. Slow down and shorten your strides as you come up to your turning point.

3. Swing your left foot over the top of the ball to fake a kick to the right, then quickly bring it back down next to the left side of the ball and a little behind. Make your fake very convincing so that the defender moves to the right. Exaggerating your body movement really helps to fake the defender.

4. Follow the fake by planting your right foot about 2 inches beyond the right side of the ball.

5. Next swivel your body 180 degrees to the left, then push the ball forward a little to the left using the inside of your right foot.

6. Now accelerate away as you complete the move

7. Remember to come into the move slow, then come out very fast.

The Rivelino Move Instructions (No.127)

1. Start by standing with both feet on the right hand side of the ball.

2. Now pivoting on your left foot quickly bring your right foot forward and over towards the ball as if you are going to move or kick the ball in that direction

3. But actually miss the ball and place your right foot about 3 inches on the left side of the ball

4. Now at the same time you are doing this, slide your left foot across the back of the ball until it's 12 inches on the other side.

5. Then the ball should be played away to the right using the outside of your right foot.

6. Next move the ball forward at a 45 degree angle in the direction you are facing.

7. Explode out by dribbling for 4 yards to finish the move.

The Matthews Move Instructions (No.128)

1. Start by standing with the ball between the toes part of your feet, which are about 12 inches apart.

2. Now touch the ball lightly with the inside of your right foot, moving it about 6 inches away slightly to the left.

3. At the same time you do that, make a big hop sideways 24 inches to the left with your left foot.

4. Make sure you dip your left shoulder as you hop.

5. Next push off with your left foot and move the ball forward to the right using the outside of your right foot.

6. Now accelerate away for about 4 yards as you complete the move.

7. To make this move more convincing, try to develop a good body fake along with a quick change of direction.

The Scissors Move Instructions (No.129)

1. Start by standing with both feet on the right hand side of the ball.

2. Now lift your left foot over the top of the ball and plant it about 12 inches to the left of the ball.

3. As you are doing this, dip your shoulders to the left to fake a move in that direction.

4. Then quickly bring your right foot around behind the ball so that you can move the ball away to the right using the outside of your right foot.

5. Now dribble the ball away forward at about a 45 degree angle for about 4 yards to finish

The Double Scissors Move Instructions (No.130)

1. Start by standing with both feet on the right hand side of the ball.

2. Now lift your left foot over the top of the ball and plant it about 12 inches to the left of the ball.

3. As you are doing this, dip your shoulders to the left to fake a move in that direction.
4. Then quickly bring your right foot around behind the ball , but don't plant it this time.
5. Instead, this time lift your right foot over the ball in the opposite direction to the right. Dip your shoulders to the right to carry out the fake.
6. As you do the scissors with your right foot bring your left foot around behind the ball. But don't plant it yet.
7. Instead, this time move the ball to the left with the outside of the left foot.
8. Now explode away forward to the left using the outside of your left foot for about 4 yards to finish the move.

The Matthews/Scissors Combo Move Instructions (No.131)

1. Start by standing with the ball between the toes part of your feet, which are about 12 inches apart.
2. Now touch the ball lightly with the inside of your right foot, moving it only about 6 inches away slightly to the left.
3. At the same time you do that, make a big hop sideways 24 inches to the left with your left foot.
4. Make sure you dip your left shoulder as you hop.
5. Next fake playing the ball with the outside of your right foot, but instead lift it up and over to the right as you would with the scissor move.
6. Now plant your right foot 12 inches to the right of the ball.
7. Next bring your left foot around behind the ball, then accelerate away forward to the left for about 4 yards using the outside of the left foot.

The Beardsley Move Instructions (No.132)

1. Start by dribbling towards a target.
2. Now reach around to the right side of the ball with the inside of your right foot big toe.
3. Then cut the ball 6 inches directly back right along the line it was traveling in.
4. Next swivel around to the left by pivoting on your right foot to face the direction from where you started. Exaggerate your body movement as you swivel back, and pretend you are turning to dribble back the way you came.

111

5. Now reverse the swivel by pivoting on your left foot back toward the front, then cut the ball forward toward your target using the inside of your right big toe again.

6. Then accelerate away fast for about 4 yards to finish the move.

The Maradona Turn Instructions (No.133)

1. Start by dribbling the ball slowly forward about 4 yards while passing it back and forth from your right foot to your left foot.

2. Place your right foot sole on top of the ball causing it to stop, then keep it there.

3. Now jump in the air, pushing up with your left foot. Rotate your body 180 degrees to the rear off your right foot while it just lightly still touches the ball.

4. Replace your right foot with your left foot on top of the ball while your body continues to spin in the air.

5. Land with your right foot planted and your left foot on top of the ball.

6. Now roll the ball in front of you with your left foot instead of lifting it like you did your right foot. The ball is now going in the opposite direction you started.

7. Next catch up to the ball and dribble it away for about 4 yards to complete the move.

The Cryuff Turn Instructions (No.134)

1. Start by dribbling the ball slowly forward about 4 yards.

2. Come up to the ball and place your left foot along the left side of the ball.

3. Now set up and fake like you are going to kick the ball with your right foot.

4. Instead of kicking it though swing your right leg over the ball and hook it around the right side until your right knee is turned inward toward your left knee.

5. Make sure you exaggerate your arm swing when you fake kicking the ball.

6. Then flick the ball behind you between your legs using the inside of your right foot.

7. Now spin quickly around to your left, keeping your body low, and looking immediately over your left shoulder for the ball.

8. Catch up to the ball, then accelerate away and dribble for about 4 yards to complete the move and finish.